I0483042

YELLOW BOXES

YELLOW BOXES

EUN HYE KIM

NEW DEGREE PRESS

COPYRIGHT © 2019 EUN HYE KIM

All rights reserved.

YELLOW BOXES

ISBN 978-1-64137-324-1 *Paperback*

978-1-64137-628-0 *Ebook*

To my mother and father, who raised me up with so much love.

Truly, I never lacked for what I needed most. Thank you.

CONTENTS

INTRODUCTION

——

Gifts are strange. Receiving a gift feels oddly touching and melancholy at the same time. *How do you love me enough to give me something?* I always wonder. There is power in the exchange of giving and receiving a gift. Gifts connote the past, where the giver brings something into the present as an accumulation of anchoring memories and moments. Gifts are also hope for the future because the receiver becomes inextricably linked to the giver. The object itself may be consumed, worn away, or lost one day, but the giver and receiver remain linked.

    I have a cousin who joined my family in the US and lived with us for six years until he got married. Fourteen years older, he was another older sibling for me. Even as a baby, I was attached to this cousin—my mom told me I would immediately stop crying when he stepped into the room. I still remember sitting at the table as a four-year-old and looking at my cousin as he ate his cereal before school. I loved the way he crunched his cereal, so different-sounding to me than his older brother next to him.

After my cousin got married, he gave me a gift on my birthday: a box in the shape of a house, and when I took off the roof, it was filled with Mentos. My family laughed at the gag gift, but I laughed a bit harder, understanding what it meant. You see, back when we lived in the same house, Mentos had been my cousin's bribes for me to do the dishes. He would negotiate with me, holding up one finger and then two if I were particularly reluctant, his bright eyes opened wide in emphasis and his smile hovering on the edge of laughter.

I laughed but also mourned for those past days that wouldn't come back. We no longer needed to negotiate between one or two Mentos. My cousin gave me a box in the shape of a house filled with Mentos. I received it because I understood.

In this story that I set out to write, I thought of wrapped gifts in particular: the beautiful spectacle of it all only to be ripped through, the impenetrable quality that heightens the suspense, and then the relief of finally opening it. I thought of what it means to give gifts to one another in a family and how that stays with us. I thought of an Auntie who desperately wants to give gifts to her girls: beautifully wrapped yellow boxes tied up in pink satin ribbon, in a Dr. Seuss-style teetering pile. Would these girls ultimately receive their gifts, and what would they find inside them?

THE HENDERSON GIRLS

—

THE ELDERS

Hana—the dancer
Dul—the wrath
Set—the swan
Net—the soother

THE MIDDLES

Da-seot—the beauty
Yeo-seot—the glutton
Il-gop—the violinist

THE LITTLES

Yeo-deol—the artist
Ahop—the sloth
Yeol—the biter

MOTHER

SEO-AH

1960

Seo-ah turned a bloated page of her book, ignoring the wet tiles soaking into her back. Rather than reading, it was more interesting to observe the bodies of the older women, *ahjum-mas* and *halmonis*, walking between the washing stations and the big bathtubs of hot and cold water. Their thickened bodies submerged and rose from the water, easing up their day's thoughts in the air. *Had the rice been washed? Had the stew tasted too bitter? Had the lipstick today been worth tomorrow's bickering?*

Understanding that her body would look like that too one day, slackened and heavy from life, Seo-ah turned the pity onto herself and returned to her book. The steam of the bathtub clung sweetly to her nose, emanating from the peeled-open yogurt containers along the wet floor that she would have to pick up later. Some of the women patted Seo-ah's hair as they passed by.

"What a smart girl. Keep on reading your books and marry a respectable Korean man one day," they said. The meaner ones spelled out the insinuation, adding, "Not like those whores who drop out of school and wiggle their chests at men."

Seo-ah smiled and said, "Thank you" to these comments, deciding to give them back their pity as they walked away. Pitiful, shallow creatures. They had allowed their bodies to become thickened by regret, and now they were lashing their resentment out on her youth.

At four in the evening, the bathhouse closed for an hour to prepare for the night crowd. Seo-ah held her breath as she reached down to the hair swirled around the drains, her least favorite task. There was always so much hair that at the end of the day, the bunched up hair in the waste bin sickened her. It looked like a decapitated head.

After checking that all the drains were unclogged, Seo-ah moved to the sparsely furnished entrance that was mostly occupied by the front desk. The straw of the worn flooring pricked into her bare feet as she organized the wooden passes into a basket, something her mother constantly forgot.

"Why don't you get some air?" her mother suggested, placing an apple on the desk.

Her mother looked like she could use the air more as she massaged her temples with her jaundiced hands. She looked pretty in a faded dress, the same murky gray that all her clothes had turned into over the years, and her shock of thick black hair was curled into its perpetual bob. The *ahjummas* loved to touch her hair and ask where she found such a dye.

The lingering look of her mother's hazel eyes on the rigid backside of her father sweeping the floor across the room gave away her mother's intentions.

Seo-ah rolled her eyes, slowly, so her mother could see, but she obediently snatched up the apple and stepped out into the December chill. She settled in her accustomed spot on the cement steps leading up to the door, as she did most evenings.

Time narrowed into the curling red apple skin she focused on peeling in a single strip, feeling her perpetually damp hair stiffen under the towel draped over her head. Her mother's moans sounded from the open windows, warming the air in that sole spot of frigid evening. Each time Seo-ah thought she heard a shuffling at the brass gates, she paused and turned the knife in her hand until the footsteps retreated.

It had only been a summer thing, but the hopefuls still showed up from time to time. The first time had been so easy, slipping through the curtain to the men's side. A low-throated chuckle—perhaps the uncle at the general store who always slipped in a free taffy candy for her, perhaps the pastor's adult son who had slipped a flower in her hair—and the drop of pants, the clang of a metal buckle on the floor. No one had stopped her. By the end of the summer, Seo-ah had been able to buy two bundles of books with the crumpled bills inside her burlap uniform.

Yes, I'll keep reading my books, she thought.

Once it fell quiet around the windows, Seo-ah stood up, irritated at all the chores there were left to do. Before heading inside, she pulled the towel out of her hair and set it down with the peeled apple on top. With a final glance back at the apple atop the towel, indiscernible in the shadows by the door, Seo-ah rolled up her sleeves and braced herself for another long night.

For hours, the heavy steam of the bathing area enveloped Seo-ah as she scrubbed the women's broad backs until they shined pink and lathered soap through the small scalps of their children. Occasionally, a baby was thrust into her arms as the overwhelmed mother winced against the soap in her eyes.

As the bathing area emptied out, Seo-ah took out her book from the bottom of the towel pile. This one was about a magical land inside a wardrobe. When the bathhouse officially closed and Seo-ah worked on draining the tubs, she stared at her pruned hand under the gray water. Was fifteen too grown-up to escape into a magical land?

When Seo-ah finally emerged back into the dark entrance, the clock hands read three in the morning. Her parents had long gone to bed. Seo-ah stepped outside and smiled.

Dong-ju lay asleep on the cement stairs with his head propped up on the towel. The core of the apple was in his outstretched hand, as if he had drifted off to sleep after eating it. Seo-ah bent down and tickled under his chin.

"Ooojju jju jju," she cooed, "your lips are going to twist funny if you sleep in the cold."

He stirred awake in slow blinks that fluttered into her heart, his eyes rounding open and letting in more light. They were honest eyes that would never betray her.

"Are you hungry?" Dong-ju asked. He picked up a cloth-covered metal tray at his feet, leftovers from his mother's restaurant. Every night, Dong-ju came to see Seo-ah after working all day at the restaurant.

"Famished," Seo-ah said, pulling him inside with a slip of her warm hand under his shirt. She would not cry like her mother did, her mother who spilled her desire out of the open windows for the whole neighborhood to hear.

Seo-ah had met Dong-ju during her summer thing when he walked up without any preamble and punched the man that she had been finishing off. The commotion drew her father inside, and Seo-ah had calmly wiped her mouth, waiting for the verbal torrent of anger and then confusion, the head shaving and disowning she heard whispered about.

"… dare you, using your fists in my bathhouse. Don't you dare come back here ever again!"

The words hadn't been directed at her. Seo-ah looked up to see Dong-ju's broad backside, blocking her perfectly from her father's line of sight.

Dong-ju was banned from returning to the bathhouse, but he returned the next night with a metal tray of carefully arrayed leftovers. An apology, only for Seo-ah. He continued to visit every night after that as summer turned into autumn, and Seo-ah didn't tell him, but she also stopped going into the men's side of the bathhouse. Rumors of the "special service" at the bathhouse, meanwhile, had belatedly spread through the neighborhood.

This first night came back to Seo-ah as she and Dong-ju fed each other, sitting inside an emptied tub afterward. Their clothes and undergarments draped off the tub's ledge like a carousel of garments.

"Why did you punch that man?" Seo-ah asked vaguely, knowing Dong-ju would understand enough.

"Because what he was doing to you was wrong," he answered plainly.

"He wasn't doing anything to me. I chose to do it, we both chose to do it," Seo-ah said.

Dong-ju hugged her to him so they faced each other chest to chest.

"You looked like you were going to cry."

Seo-ah covered his eyes, not wanting him to see the fresh tears on her cheeks. The moment passed in silence, and she dropped her hands to lean in for a kiss, a kiss of gratitude. They turned their focus back on picking out the edible parts of the food on the tray, an assortment of lipstick-smudged vegetable pancakes and half-bitten fried chicken.

"Mom hates those whores who cake their faces with makeup for a meal, but at least someone's paying for them," Dong-ju said in a direct parroting of his mother's dialect to make Seo-ah laugh.

She slapped his cheek.

"Your mom is a whore too," Seo-ah said.

Dong-ju sucked the grease on his fingers, unable to hide the spreading flush of deep-bitten embarrassment. He was trying, Seo-ah understood, and the depth of his empathy often stunned her like it had the first night. Yet in his lapses of consideration, she was unrelenting in punishing him, as if he had finally proven her worst fears. Dong-ju accepted it all, and Seo-ah never wanted to let go of him. And she hoped he would never let go of her. Seo-ah gathered his hands into hers and closed her eyes.

"Take us somewhere very, very far away from here," she whispered in a half-lidded invocation to the boy she held.

1961

The winter evenings of her fifteenth year passed peacefully with Dong-ju.

In the spring, Seo-ah turned sixteen with seaweed soup and freshly prepared *banchan*, side dishes of kimchi shredded in long pieces, bean sprouts and spinach stir-fried in sesame oil, and slices of Spam fried in egg batter. Her mother set the food out in their nice china rimmed with blue flowers.

"You'd never believe it, but I saw a girl who looked just like you at the market!" Seo-ah's mother said as she poured barley tea into their glasses. Her father was slow to arrive at the table in his usual manner of waking up.

Seo-ah scooped up a spoonful of rice into her mouth and busied herself with tracing the flowers on her plate. She didn't find it worth answering her mother, who had a lot of mistaken daughters from the market. At the silence, Seo-ah looked up to see her mother's expectant gaze.

The hazel of her mother's eyes, jarring against her black hair, impressed a false sense of un-Korean exoticness that belied her weak vision. When the light fell at a certain slant on some mornings, the hazel took on a translucence and Seo-ah would become aware of how keenly her mother stared with her fingers dug into her bottom lip. It was like her mother emptied her body to occupy a different, surely better place than the wearying monotony of their life.

Seo-ah hated her mother the most in these moments. *Take me with you,* a childish voice within her whispered, the part of her that searched for her mother's hand in the dark.

"Let's take a picture of the birthday girl with her birthday feast," her father said, approaching the table. His black eyes bore into Seo-ah with the determination that made young girls and some boys flush, though her father would be oblivious to his effect. The nose that looked so broad on Seo-ah's face anchored her father's handsome features. Seo-ah's mother joined him, leaning into the novelty of the camera he held in his hands.

Together, they fit perfectly.

"No, *appa*—" Seo-ah protested to her father, still wearing her pajama shirt, a soft buttery yellow button-up that Dong-ju had given her, his favorite.

Her father wasn't listening, raising up the camera to his eye.

"Three..."

Seo-ah straightened her back. She didn't want to waste the film, she told herself.

"Two..."

Unsure where to look, her eyes roamed around for the center of the lens.

"One."

The shutter clicked, washing everything out in the white of the flash.

Seo-ah blinked against her disorientation, first making out her father's right hand on her mother's narrow waist, then his furrowed brow tracing some perpetual frustration, and the bloom of light in her mother's hazel cornea that leached her eyes totally white.

"Careful." Seo-ah's father caught her from slipping off the chair.

The camera on his neck swung in a neat arc and bashed into the table. Her father cursed as he gingerly picked it up, wetting his thumb to rub along the white scratches.

"Deok-su," her mother chided her father, but she was laughing.

Her mother's hands hovered around his face, caught between wanting to cover up his mouth and touching his cheek, and her father looked so happy as he pushed his chin into her hands, ending her mother's dilemma. Seo-ah took in the scene and squeezed her eyes closed. This would be the photograph she kept for herself.

Two hours after her birthday officially passed, Seo-ah opened the front door.

The tension from the day of work melted away as she took in the flowers clustered around Dong-ju, who was fast asleep, and along each cement step leading up to her in an array of red, white, and purple blossoms. It was like a page out of a beautiful picture book, a book that wasn't hers to read. Seo-ah stepped carefully around the flowers to lay down next to Dong-ju, resting her cheek on the cool stone of the step.

"Where did you get all these flowers?" she asked.

"Happy birthday," Dong-ju said, smiling, his eyes still closed.

"It's already past my birthday, and I know you can't afford flowers like this."

"Can't you just say thank you?"

Seo-ah pressed her nose into Dong-ju's chest, feeling the bob of his throat above her head trying to quell down the hurt.

"That's not you and me. We meet, we fuck, we eat your mom's leftovers, and repeat," she said softly.

Seo-ah pushed off his shoulders for the physical distance, to get away from the pain she was inflicting onto him. Dong-ju sat up and scrambled his hair in exasperation.

"Why can't we change? This is a proper gift. Those GI girls are always passing by lugging huge bouquets of flowers. I thought you would be happy."

"Happy?" Seo-ah asked.

The inflection of doubt smothered the air between them. Dong-ju turned to Seo-ah, his eyes frozen on her, yet all the surrounding flowers were reflected back to her in his black irises.

"What do you want from me?" he asked. Each word quivered with a desperation dredged up from the soul.

Seo-ah gripped her hands in her lap. *I want to stop hurting you.* But she had to tell him the truth, the resolve she had nourished inside her since the night she took Dong-ju's hands and spoke the invocation for escape.

"I want to leave, go somewhere far, far away, together with you. Remember? I want to begin our own lives, Dong-ju, away from all this. I want to be happy with you—I don't need you to *make* me happy," Seo-ah said breathlessly.

"Leave?" Dong-ju laughed bitterly. "What about my *umma*?"

Seo-ah squared her shoulders, hitting the biggest obstacle in her scheme: Dong-ju's mother. They had never met each other, but the sentiment was clear enough as the leftovers he brought increasingly began to smell like vinegar, which Dong-ju's dull sense of smell couldn't make out but soured everything in Seo-ah's mouth that she chewed thoroughly for Dong-ju.

"What about the restaurant?" Dong-ju stood up and backed down the stairs, each step further from Seo-ah squeezing her chest.

"I can't just leave and play house with you. Maybe it's easy for you because your parents have each other, but my *umma* would be all alone. I'd be no better than my *appa* then."

Dong-ju spit at the ground, as if the word for dad, *appa*, dirtied his mouth. Seo-ah had never heard him refer to his dad following a terse debriefing that his dad had left him and his mom eight years ago for another woman.

He asked one last question before exiting the brass gates.

"You make these demands of me, but what have you done for me?"

Seo-ah braced herself for the clang of the gates that would wake up her parents, yet it never came. When she looked up, the gate was in its place under Dong-ju's ever-gentle hand. He left her alone with the bloom of flowers, like they had magically bloomed through the cement.

Seo-ah picked up a white flower and touched the petals. Tissue paper. Beneath the paper, the metal wires twisted in the meticulous skeleton of the flowers that had looked so lifelike, like the flowers Seo-ah had never been able to see in real life.

It must have been agonizing on Dong-ju's fingers to twist and shape the wire for each flower. Yet as Seo-ah piled the paper flowers onto the top step, she knew that didn't explain the perfume lingering on Dong-ju's neck, or from where he had conjured the beautiful tissue paper.

The summer and fall evenings of her sixteenth year passed without Dong-ju.

The gates remained unlocked, but Seo-ah couldn't bring herself to go out the door anymore. His question weighed on her throughout the months: "What have you done for me?"

"I can do nothing for you," Seo-ah repeated to herself, facing the darkened entrance room. She only had her useless dreams of faraway places.

Dong-ju didn't give up. He knew Seo-ah well enough to read into the meaning of the unlocked gate, because he came every night still and sat on the stairs until the sun came up. Some nights, he slept on a pillow Seo-ah left outside for him, and other nights, when the sky was clearer, he talked as if he could sense she was right there on the other side of the door.

He always began with an apology, the apology that Seo-ah was working to form on her end, and filled in the silence of the night with confessions that only accumulated and added to the existing weight in her heart.

"I'm sorry, Seo-ah. All those things I said to you, they weren't your burden to bear."

"Just give me a sign if you don't want me to come like this."

"I love you even though it's hard to understand you a lot of times."

"That first night, I noticed the contempt in your eyes first. You couldn't have been a prostitute with eyes like that, I thought. Surely it was a mistake that you were sitting in the corner by the men's tub. But the man approached you and you let him shove your head down. I recognized it immediately in the blur of your eyes, the grit of your teeth. You were just trying to survive."

"You really did look like you were going to cry.

It felt like you were looking directly at me.

Maybe you were looking for someone, for anyone."

Dong-ju continued to bring food, which he left in the shadows by the front door, underneath the pillow. The food shifted from his mother's leftovers doused in vinegar to clumsy food obviously made by Dong-ju: a loose roll of kimbap that fell apart in Seo-ah's hand, thin omelet sleeves tearing with rice, burnt sweet potatoes. Seo-ah loved all of it, thought it felt wrong to accept his food while she continued faltering to face him.

On the second dawn of December, Seo-ah peeked outside the door after hearing the soft clang of the gates closing behind Dong-ju. The pillow she left for him to use rested on its side instead of lying flat over the food as usual. Thinking that was strange, Seo-ah lifted the pillow. *Dugun...Dugun...Dugun.* Her heart fluttered, looking down at a pink frosted cake.

Seo-ah had only heard about cake, what the Americans ate on their birthdays. Much too sweet to finish a single slice, yet Dong-ju had baked her a whole cake. In the kitchen window, the sky was starting to lighten as she crouched on the floor and cut out a sliver of the cake. It was red bean on the inside. Seo-ah laughed at the ridiculousness of a red bean cake slathered in American frosting. Her private breakfast tasted of red bean and the salt of her tears.

As her parents' quiet sighs grew restless upstairs, waking up into one another, Seo-ah slid the cake in the back of the freezer. The morning was slow at the bathhouse, and at four in the evening, Seo-ah accepted the small change her parents pushed onto her to go buy an ice cream bar, never mind that it was winter. Slipping on a green sweater over her burlap uniform, Seo-ah settled on the front steps with her cake.

Preoccupied with licking up globs of frosting, Seo-ah didn't notice the opening of the gate and the tentative shuffling of someone's shoes.

"Excuse me, miss, is the bathhouse open?" a male voice asked in English.

Seo-ah looked up, landing in a vague sense of the words from the books she had read.

An American man stood in his uniform, holding a plastic basket of shampoo and soap in the crook of his arm like the *ahjummas* and *halmonis*. He looked older, around her father's age, with brown hair curling into his bewildered gray eyes as Seo-ah laughed at him, a giant American holding a bath basket like any other Korean person.

The look in his eyes didn't change as he stepped closer, and Seo-ah's laughter halted, taking in how much larger he was, remembering the rumors that swirled throughout the neighborhood.

"No kiss kiss," Seo-ah spat, inching up the stairs, but she stopped.

There was something peculiar happening in the man's eyes that had remained locked on her the whole time. Like the dispelling of rain clouds, his gray eyes seemed to lighten. Seo-ha looked at the overcast sky behind him but glimpsed no sun or break in the clouds for such a change.

The man raised up his right arm, and then his left arm in surrender.

"No kiss kiss," he agreed, and then slower, so she could understand his English, "I came here for a bath, you know, to become clean."

The man mimed scrubbing his back and hair awkwardly. All his movements seemed to be fraught in an anxiousness that Seo-ah didn't understand, so unlike the men who frequented the bathhouse, and Dong-ju, until she also noticed the flush spreading down his neck.

He was flustered.

"Where your eyes?" Seo-ah asked him in English, hearing the clash of her pronunciation.

Where do you come from with eyes like yours?

The man's eyes widened, as if he had been caught doing something wrong. "My eyes are right here. I'm looking at you. I can see you." His words spilled out, panicked.

Seo-ah frowned, taking it that she had asked the wrong question. "Where you?" Seo-ah tried again, drawing out the shape of a house with her finger.

"My house?" The man calmed down. "I live two neighborhoods over. But I'm going to make my home somewhere far, far away," the man answered, his expectant gaze searing on Seo-ah.

He could have said anything, but the words *far, far away* dropped down Seo-ah's throat, wriggling the weight inside her chest.

Take me with you.

Without further conversation, Seo-ah pointed him to the men's side, letting him overpay to bathe in the grimy water floating with dead skin and hair. She knew he would return tomorrow, and the day after that. Then, she would slacken her coldness toward him.

When it was five o'clock in the evening and the man had left, Seo-ah left the pink cake in the shadowed part by the door. Later that night, she passed the door of the entrance room and slept in her own bed, hugging the yellow button-down in her arms.

1962

On the first day of January, Seo-ah accepted the man's proposal for marriage.

His name was Alan. Once her visa was prepared, they left for the US. In her suitcase, Seo-ah slipped in the tissue paper flowers and the yellow button-down. The cab pulled up in front of the bathhouse in the early morning just as the darkened sky lit up, like she had instructed Alan, who caught her sliding into her seat with a kiss.

Seo-ah's last thought before take-off was Dong-ju, who would continue to sit on her steps until someone told him. She could already see the words of denial forming on his lips.

Whore, whore, whore.

PROLOGUE

———

There were seven before Yeo-deol, and two after her. People often asked them if their mother had died in childbirth by their sheer number. They would reply they had no mother because they didn't know how to explain where they came from.

Yeo-deol had a real name, though she seldom used it among her sisters, who also collectively ignored their given names to go instead by Korean numbers. Her name, Yeo-deol, was *eight* in Korean, as in the eighth in the order of Henderson girls: Hana, Dul, Set, Net, Da-seot, Yeo-seot, Il-gop, Yeo-deol, Ahop, Yeol. Harsh names in monosyllabic parts to choke over, followed by sheer bewilderment to reach the *Henderson* at the end.

These numbers as names were simpler for the sisters. Their given names had disappeared the winter Mama had left the family twenty-four years ago.

Yeo-deol touched the clip in her hair, turning her head in the mirrored reflection before yanking the clip out again. She had cut her black hair last week to touch just under her ears, which looked childish now compared to her red lips. A green dress with puffed-out sleeves lay draped on the chair next to her, atop a note from Da-seot, her fifth sister.

"From the winter/spring collection...love you."

Yeo-deol's sisters were gathering tonight for her birthday.

"Wow, all your sisters?" Yeo-deol's longtime art curator had asked with rounded eyes, knowing how many they numbered. "That's so nice. You all must be close."

"Not really. It's because I'm turning twenty-nine," Yeo-deol had replied and then turned back to unwrapping the cloth binding her most recent paintings, already tired of the conversation.

Mama had been twenty-nine years old when she went away. She didn't return after the winter to turn thirty with them in spring. It felt odd to reach the same age as Mama, an oddness that sat in the chest. "I can't breathe," Hana, the oldest Henderson sister, had whispered into the phone on her twenty-ninth birthday to Yeo-deol. "Something is ballooning and burning in my chest, and it hurts so much. I want to rip everything off." The call broke off with Hana's heaving and strangers' voices of concern falling over her.

For Dul's twenty-ninth birthday, all the sisters had sat in Dul's city condo and drank their orange juice wordlessly around a cake no one ate. Dul smoked through a pack of cigarettes alone on the veranda, using her knuckles to brush away the tears that continued to come.

Yeo-deol held up a hand to her eyes against the expanse of windows letting in the morning light. She had specifically requested windows to encircle the dressing room, emulating the sleeping room of their old family estate. The only sound punctuating the silence of the room was the clock at half past ten in the morning.

Tick. Tick. Tick.

Dust stirred in the sunlight. Yeo-deol closed her eyes against the ticking of the clock wrenching into her head.

Twenty-four years ago, Yeo-deol had been five years old when Mama disappeared in a winter that remained preserved in the recesses of her mind. It always began with lines that took the shape of the old family estate, enshrouded by a shock of snow. The snow would fall away to their beautiful house that loomed with dimension, a three-story brick structure with the roof weathered to a teal blue and the rounded glass turret of the girls' sleeping room in front.

Daddy would be leaning on the table in the dining room as Schumann echoed throughout the house from the open doors of the ballroom. Inside the ballroom, Yeo-seot stood over the record player, anxious to change the record she held in her hands spotted with fingerprints greased from apple strudel. Beneath the crystal chandelier, Hana's body revolved, supported by her pointed toe.

Drowsily, Yeo-deol fluttered her eyes open to the skin of Mama's neck, Mama who had slipped into the blankets and patted out a lullaby on Yeo-deol's chest. It was a Korean lullaby that Yeo-deol couldn't understand, like most words on a Korean tongue. The shape of the words seemed to slip into the air. Behind them, the open windows poured in the white light of unripe sun and stuffed heat. Yeo-deol curled her small body tighter into Mama. "My Soo-ah, are you awake now?" Mama asked.

On the other side of Yeo-deol lay Auntie, sleeping with limp breaths. She could feel Auntie by her radiant body heat. Yeo-deol blinked and broke into a wail muffled into Mama's shoulders. "Shhh baby, I'm right here," Mama said, "You just have to know where to look."

The light faded around them. Mama's hand stopped over Yeo-deol's chest, a weight that spread up to her eyes in unwilling sleep.

Tick. Tick. Tick.

CHAPTER 1

———

Yeo-deol opened her eyes. Her heartbeat loomed over the darkened room, *du-gun...du-gun...du-gun...*

Snow smudged onto the sloping roof of the glass turret. Yeo-deol shivered, packed in the long row of her sisters' bodies. Through the surrounding glass, her eyes fixed to the black sky that expanded and curved around the falling spots of white, threatening to break through and swallow them all. "The darkness swallows up little girls to a nowhere place where you cry all you want, but there's only silence," Dul, her second oldest sister's constant threat whispered above the girls' breaths. Yeo-deol squirmed out of the blanket tucked tightly under her, as Mama did to each girl down the row nightly.

"Mama," Yeo-deol croaked, crawling over the blanket lumps of her sleeping sisters. Net's hand instinctively wrapped around Yeo-deol's forearm, which Yeo-deol gently loosened finger by finger. Balls of peppermint candies stolen from the maids rolled out from Net's sleeve. Yeo-deol dug her knee into Dul's stomach, smiling at her sleep-drowsy whine of pain. The curve of her spine still stung from the presses of Dul's cigarette butt.

The path down the long hallway and spiraling stairs was unlit, meaning it must have been late. Yeo-deol felt her way along the walls, shivering at the chill through her cotton nightgown. Her body still emanated the shared warmth of her sisters, but their house was cold no matter how many windows the girls found to close.

A square of light edged out from the kitchen. Sighs of soft laughter whispered into Yeo-deol's ears as she stepped into the light with a thumb in her mouth.

Mama and Daddy hugged one another on the counter, a human contour amidst amber bottles and cups sloshing over with pink and golden liquids. Daddy's pants spooled down around his ankles as he thrust up to his toes like Hana danced before they went to sleep. "Listen, listen," she had insisted, dancing to silence as her long sweeping arms caressed the air into secret shapes.

Mama's green slippers hung from her feet crossed around Daddy's waist. Her dress was peeled back at the front, where Daddy took his turn like Ahop and Yeol, the littles, used to do. He spoke into her chest in animal whimpers, not seeing how Mama looked down at him through her thick black hair.

Yeo-deol saw Mama. The whine of "Mama" stopped in Yeo-deol's throat. This was not her Mama. This Mama's features were hardened from the line of her jaw to the set of her eyes resembling the black chasm that Yeo-deol left behind in the turret with her sleeping sisters. Mama's eyes were the center of the kitchen that was already blurring and distorting on the edges as Yeo-deol rubbed at her own eyes, trying to pin down the familiar objects and colors. This Mama's hollowed eyes watched Daddy, who continued to rock into Mama, shaking the whole of her body and the heels of the green slippers.

Only when Daddy raised his head to touch his forehead to hers did Mama's lashes flutter closed. With a wretched contortion of her face, Mama let out a lush note that wavered in the air. Something dripped between Mama and Daddy onto the marble floor, just as Yeo-deol began to cry, clutching at the seat of her nightgown. She had wet herself. Mama opened her eyes and smiled radiantly at Yeo-deol with ongoing tears.

Mama, why do you hurt so?

The next morning, Yeo-deol lay shivering in the muted morning light underneath her blankets long after her sisters had risen. On the way out, Dul had reached in to pinch Yeo-deol's skin, whispering, "Did you think I wouldn't know it'd been you last night?"

Yeo-deol traced the yellow blemish that would eventually bruise to a purple she couldn't mix with her paint colors.

She was still full of the chocolate chip cookies and warm milk that she and Mama had quietly eaten hours before as Daddy dozed dumb to the world on the ground with his pants still slumped halfway down his legs.

"Paint me another one of your pictures tomorrow," Mama had said as she and Yeo-deol walked up the stairs together. "I love how you draw the world, our keen-eyed artist."

It was only when Net crawled into Yeo-deol's space and tugged on her hand that Yeo-deol let the blanket fall away. Net waited, swaying on her toes, as Yeo-deol found someone's sweater to pull on over her nightgown. If Yeo-deol strained her ears harder, she would hear the constant clatter of peppermint candies along a secret hem of Net's skirt.

The dining room was silent as Net and Yeo-deol entered. Yeo-deol sat in her seat at the long table. At each seat, there was a cup of black coffee and an empty plate. Breakfast, Mama's meal, was usually an aromatic selection of cream soups, sliced fruit, thinly stacked pancakes, and wrapped treats.

"Daddy, Mama said if we drink coffee, we won't grow." Yeo-seot sniffed timidly at the dark liquid.

"Is Mama sick?" Set asked with her direct gaze, her arms crossed over on the table. There was a hesitant anxiety beneath her indifferent tone.

"Mama's never overslept," Hana said, twisting her head about the dining room as if to catch Mama hiding, something to explain this anomaly.

The elders and middles all began to chatter while Daddy looked out the long windows facing the front lawn of the estate. Maids were spread out on the lawn, running back and forth to one another. Yeo-deol saw the tension straining down Daddy's hands clutched behind his back.

Finally, Il-gop slammed her hands down on the table. "I'm hungry," she said simply.

Daddy turned around to the girls as if realizing they were there for the first time. His brown hair stuck up on one side, and he ran his hand through it once more as his gray eyes darted between the ten girls. Patting his pockets with a frown, Daddy took out a key and slid it to Hana on the table.

"This is the key to the dessert pantry. Until Mama gets better, you girls help yourselves. The maids will be busy today, so stay out of their way."

With that, Daddy stepped out of the dining room. Hana closed her hand around the key before any of other girls could reach for it. The dessert pantry was where Mama packed fresh cakes and pies, usually for Daddy's continuing stream of friends throughout the house. "Too rich for little girl's tongues," Mama had said once, taking back the key the girls had succeeded in getting their hands on for a few fleeting seconds.

"Everyone upstairs to the sleeping room," Hana declared. The girls emptied out from the dining room, Net pulling a lethargic Yeo-deol by the hand. If Mama was sick this morning and the maids were occupied on the lawn, why had Daddy taken the effort to set out empty plates and full cups of coffee?

In the turret, the girls settled on their blankets that had been twisted aside. Hana stood in the middle with a straightened back, like a skinny sergeant major in her satin long-sleeve pajamas. The other girls, including Yeo-deol, unconsciously straightened their backs. Net held the youngest, Yeol, who napped in her arms. Red teeth marks ringed the crook of Net's neck from Yeol's angry mouth. Ahop was nowhere to be seen.

Hana raised up the pantry key with an air of importance. "As Daddy said, this is the key to Mama's pantry," Hana said, "and today, it's in my hands. Since there are ten of us, and who knows how many desserts in the pantry, I'm going to make it into a fun game. Whoever does the best favor for me can get a whole minicake—you know, the one Mama makes for our birthdays."

Hana spoke as if she had been able to see into the contents of the pantry despite just having received the key on Daddy's whim. Dul and Set were unimpressed and went downstairs. Stepping away from the cluster of her sisters too, Yeo-deol went to the ballroom on the first floor, still feeling last night's late cookies that had hardened into nausea. From behind the heavyset curtains that kept the ballroom in shade, Yeo-deol could hear the maids outside as she hopped around the floor in light steps to ease her stomach.

Yeo-deol slipped under a curtain to press her forehead to the window. The ballroom faced the backyard of the estate, opposite the dining room. The maids in their blue dresses were spread out across the vast green, bent under trees and picking through bushes. Daddy stood in the center of the commotion, running his hand through his hair again and again.

Yeo-deol slid down from the window to sit on the floor with her back to the window. Her gaze caught a small hand peeking from the next curtain. Yeo-deol smiled and lifted the curtain fold. Ahop slept there, suckling her thumb. Her brown hair was pasted back from her forehead as if it had been several days since she had bathed. It might as well have been since no one could find Ahop when they needed to.

After dozing off with Ahop under the curtain, Yeo-deol awoke to rough grunts and pitched screams. She slipped out from the curtain to see Da-seot and Yeo-seot wrestling one another at the entrance of the ballroom, competing to be the one who would put on Hana's dancing music. A record was already shattered into pieces on the ground.

Hana had already taken her place in the center of the ballroom to Il-gop's rapid strains of a Bach Minuet. For a moment, Hana turned with a look of serenity to Yeo-deol that seemed to suggest the pantry would be Yeo-deol's if only she got closer. Yeo-deol passed by the stupidity of her sisters to paint inside the turret. Gradually, the page gave way to a scene of green grass and the blue dots of maids.

Dinner that night was silent as the girls eagerly filled up their empty stomachs, except Hana who ate in small bites and exchanged discreet smiles with Il-gop, who aimlessly sifted the cut pieces of her steak around her plate. Yeo-deol noticed how Daddy did not comment on the fact that the girls wore their sleep clothes still. Daddy did not check on Ahop either, whose face was dipped into the soup asleep until a maid fussed over her in alarm. Mama would have done all these things. Daddy did not talk at all, methodically bringing up a spoonful of soup to his mouth. The maids weaved about the dining room bearing platters and trays with not a laugh or affectionate comment to the girls, anxious by the absence of the young mistress.

Yeo-deol sat at the dining table first the next morning, confirming her worst fear. Cups of black coffee and empty plates lined the table once again. Yeo-deol took her seat as the other girls filled their own seats with tentative steps. Daddy entered last, wearing yesterday's white button-up shirt and slacks, but his hair was combed through neatly this time. He cleared his throat, his eyes focused on an empty corner of the room.

"Mama has gone on a trip," Daddy said. "If you're all good girls, she may come back early, maybe by spring when the flowers bloom."

Yeo-deol pinched Net at the obvious lie. Even Dul scoffed softly under her breath, though she stared into her lap. Mama didn't go on trips, she seldom left the house, and that had been the way as long as the girls could remember.

However, Daddy didn't wait for questions, leaving the dining room in hard-stepped strides.

"What does it mean to be 'good'?" Yeo-seot asked. "Does that mean we were bad? Is that why Mama has gone on a trip without us?"

Yeo-deol and all the girls watched as Hana deliberated the question carefully.

"I have to think more on that, but to begin with, we have to drink our coffees. Daddy is making us appreciate all that we have by taking it away from us," Hana pronounced.

Hana picked up her cup of coffee and took a sip, sweeping a look at her sisters. Dul and Set followed, glancing at each other, and then the remaining five girls also drank their coffee. All the girls looked at one another over the brim of their cups to make sure they were finishing their coffee to the last drop, despite how it scalded their tongues and tasted more pungent than its color. Yeo-seot began to cry at her empty plate, hungry as she always was, inconsolable even when Da-seot offered her cup.

Yeo-deol swirled the coffee in her mouth. She sensed Daddy would punish them until Mama returned, or until one of the girls' stomachs shriveled up from the bitterness.

CHAPTER 2

———

The elder and middle girls dispersed at the base of the staircase after breakfast to their individual occupations.

Hana announced that there would be performance of *Sleeping Beauty* tomorrow night and pulled away Da-seot and Yeo-seot to the ballroom by their wrists. Da-seot because she was the prettiest with her pure eyes, wavy black hair, and delicately shaped nose; Yeo-seot as the only girl who could aptly pick through Daddy's classical music record collection.

"Whoever else joins in can get their pick from the pantry!" Hana's voice echoed down the hallway. Even Dul and Set paused momentarily on their way upstairs, their arms draped over tight stomachs. With a shake of their heads, though, they proceeded upstairs in their quiet way. Il-gop had already disappeared with her violin cradled in her arms.

Net led Yeo-deol into Mama's dressing room on the fourth floor to see what clothes she had taken with her. Mama always had the most breathtaking dresses: flowers that seemed to be trapped into the lace still alive, jeweled beadwork from which Mama had to swat away their little fingers angled to pick out bits for themselves, and fabrics that changed from one light to another. New dresses arrived to the house often in plastic sleeves and tissue paper smelling of perfume. There weren't any gaps in the swelling of gowns and dresses on the racks, however, as Net pushed Yeo-deol on the wheeled ladder along the closet.

At the dresser top, Net counted the perfume bottles, pausing only to dump the nearly empty ones onto the lap of her skirt. "Mama has thirty-three bottles of perfumes total," Net said. Yeo-deol nodded, trusting Net, who obsessively counted her possessions and those of others she stole from, as if to assure herself that she was the only one stealing from them. The only person Net didn't steal from was Mama.

Yeo-deol skimmed her hands over Mama's shoes on the floor. She couldn't count as sharply as Net, yet from the color pattern that Yeo-deol picked out in the organization of the shoes, between the honey-hued glass heels Mama sometimes wore to church on Sundays and the azure flats that glinted only in direct light, she noticed that the greens slippers Mama wore the night before were missing.

As Net tried out the handles of several drawers, none of which yielded to her pulls, Yeo-deol curled her whole body over the shoes and listened to the distant Tchaikovsky sounding from the ballroom below. Sometimes the waltz would stop abruptly, and Hana would begin yelling: "What is *wrong* with you today?"

Later, Yeo-deol passed by the ballroom hand-in-hand with Net. They were headed to the maids' quarters on the ground floor to play Net's favorite game of treasure that would turn up chocolate balls filled with berry filling and unsuspecting pastel slips of bookmarks from which Net read impassioned confessions of love. In the corner of the shadowed ballroom, Yeo-deol saw Yeo-seot with her head bowed over the record player, tensely squeezing her jutting arms. Yeo-seot looked like she would die, the anxiety of hunger hurting her physically. She constantly had something to gnaw on, and during meals, she was the only one aside from Daddy who ate in second and third servings. Yeo-deol vowed to save a chocolate ball for Yeo-seot, if she remembered not to eat all of them.

In the span of a week, the girls' regular routines fractured in quiet ways. It was implicitly understood among the maids that they would not infringe on breakfast, Mama's meal. They could only hover around the wall of the dining room, and any sigh or sound of pity that passed through their lips was reprimanded by ten pairs of resentful eyes. Da-seot played her records late into the night, casting the following silence in an eeriness that made Yeo-deol grip her covers tighter.

As if to offset the bitterness of the girls' empty break-fasts, crooked and bland-tasting pastries made by the maids' clumsy hands piled the dining table between meals. Only Da-seot tentatively picked from the pile to fill her hunger. Yeo-deol would sit at the table to sketch the crumbling bread and runny cream, and look up to see Da-seot or Il-gop looking in with disdain low on their brow.

At night, the girls split between sleeping in the glass turret and sleeping in the ballroom. Hana, Da-seot, and Yeo-seot had taken to camping in the ballroom along with Il-gop. The remaining girls stayed in the turret: Yeo-deol slept in a loose cluster with Net and the two littles, and Dul and Set on the other end of the turret.

Tomorrow never seemed to come as Hana kept pushing back the *Sleeping Beauty* performance. The practices would disintegrate each day at the moment when the performance seemed to begin. Yeo-deol sometimes laid out on the cool ballroom floor with her sketchbook and could gradually begin to anticipate the moment that infuriated Hana. The first time that Yeo-deol saw it, Da-seot, who played the beautiful princess, began the practice with difficulty. She stumbled over simple lines and her stiff dancing lacked to Hana's, faltering into uncertainty for the next move. Yeo-deol smudged black charcoal onto her paper for the despair that touched the edges of Da-seot's turns and spilled out of her eyes.

Either oblivious or pretending to be, Hana called out "Again!" at each stumbled move. Hana was patient, though, and used an encouraging tone with her struggling actress, explaining how to remember a dance sequence: "It's like gathering yourself back to your body as it escapes from you … Think of it like narrowing your mind into a single thread, and you move with only that."

Nothing worked, and eventually, Hana called for a break. "I want you to watch me carefully," she said, stepping into Da-seot's part effortlessly.

Da-seot didn't pay attention. She drew her shoulders as if seized with pain down her spine, and pressed the palm of her hands to her eyes, her rattling breaths quieting into a strange *tick tick tick* that unnerved Ye-deol. The other girls trickled into the room, sensing that something was about to erupt. Hana looked on without making a move to help her sister until Yeo-deol clambered up to soothe her exhausted sister. Prying away Da-seot's hands from her face, Yeo-deol gasped softly.

In the time that had elapsed behind her hands, Da-seot's usually bright gaze, framed by her long lashes, had dimmed to a sober dignity. When Hana indifferently resumed their practice, Da-seot's pink mouth formed around words that made the onlooking girls' hearts flutter and ache for this poor soul who had been cursed from birth—so beautiful, so kind, so forbearing a princess—and the girls turned their heated eyes to the witch, Hana, whose arms were spread in a magnificent dance that seemed to be summoning the devil. Hana, who was not as immersed as Da-seot, could no longer endure the humiliation and marched over to pinch the flesh on Da-seot's neck. Da-seot yelped, returning back to their ordinary sister. Yeo-deol and the other girls quietly left the ballroom, leaving Da-seot to cry as her oldest sister tore the flowers out of her hair.

"I'm sorry," Da-seot wailed, not knowing for what exactly she was apologizing.

After seven mornings of empty plates and black coffee, Auntie visited the girls for the first time. On that eighth night, Yeo-deol and Net had been sweeping through the vast space of the third floor after dinner, the only floor not sectioned into rooms, trying to find Ahop. They passed by Dul, who stood with Set by the open window with their hair wet, examining the new pack of cigarettes in its wrapping that Dul had stolen from Daddy's study.

The familiar chime of "Für Elise" rang through the house. Someone was at the door. The girls halted in the echoes of Daddy's booming footsteps to the front door. "Mama," Set breathed, dropping the box of cigarettes out the window.

Dul, Set, Net, and Yeo-deol ran to the stairway and struggled with their bodies choked at the landing between the handrails, grabbing at one another to get through first. Yeo-deol yanked Dul aside by her hair, satisfaction curdling in her stomach as Dul's head jerked backward with an ugly grunt. Crawling under Net, whose legs were braced against Set's frantic pushing, Yeo-deol ran downstairs to the clatter of her teeth, already picturing Mama standing at the front door wearing some flowing gown in a soft lemon color and bearing presents from wherever she had gone.

Heaving with heavy breaths, Yeo-deol dropped down to a squat at the base of the stairs. Daddy's figure blocked the person at the door. He spoke in a tone too low to be made out, but Yeo-deol recognized the sloping tension that usually preceded punishment for the girls. Beyond the door, snow fell densely from the softened night sky, accumulating in a fresh powdering of snow in the foyer's entrance. Yeo-deol tilted her head to the right to peek around Daddy.

Hazel eyes. Mama's eyes were dark, like her black hair.

The hazel eyes drifted around the dimly lit foyer and settled on Yeo-deol. A woman moved past Daddy's shoulder as he yelled, "What the hell do you think you're doing?" Daddy turned around fiercely, and the girls tensed, drawing closer to each other. Daddy's face was clenched with an emotion that Yeo-deol had never seen before. It cut into the furrow of his brow and stuffed his mouth with something hard. The veins in his neck seemed to be working up the force to spit out what was bared between his teeth.

Many years later, Yeo-deol would find the word for it: *rage*.

The woman looked like Mama drawn out in sharper lines. And the wrong colors. She stopped at the base of the stairwell and bent down to Yeo-deol's level. Yeo-deol rubbed at her eyes as her chest ached in false recognition. The Mama-like person's black hair was shorn short, and she wore a green sweater with draping sleeves and jean pants.

"Mama?" Da-seot whispered next to Yeo-deol. Set's hands came over Da-seot's mouth and nose to silence her, leaving Da-seot to frantically tap for breath.

"Daddy must have shaved Mama's head and locked her outside for going on a trip without telling him," Hana whispered more quietly for the other girls to hear. Yeo-deol shook her head slowly. Couldn't Hana see that this wasn't their mother?

"You must be Yeo-deol, the artist," the woman began. "I'm your Auntie, from your Mama's side. I've wanted to meet you and your sisters for a very long time."

Dugun…Dugun…Dugun.

Before Yeo-deol could answer, she was crushed into a spinning hug. Yeo-deol suffocated for breath against the front of the woman's sweater that was wet with melted snow. It wasn't until Daddy yanked her out of Auntie's hold that Yeo-deol could breathe again. Yeo-deol reveled in the dusty air of the foyer as a ripping pain seared up her arm from the force of the pull.

"Look, Yeo-deol's crying. The Auntie hurt her," Net said. Frigid air blew in from the open door behind Auntie, whose arms were paused in the emptied embrace. The girls gathered tightly around Daddy and Yeo-deol in an artifice of solidarity. Yeo-deol kept her head down, feeling her warm tears dot Daddy's shoulder as she waited for her heart to settle.

"Get out," Daddy bit out. The heat of Daddy's throat warmed Yeo-deol's ear.

"This isn't how it was supposed to be," Yeo-deol heard the Auntie say faintly. "I know everything about my girls."

"Get out," Daddy repeated again. Yeo-deol followed the slope of Daddy's shoulder down to his outstretched arm shielding the girls from Auntie. The girls bunched together behind this protective arm, eagerly falling into the mechanics of the drama playing out before them. "I don't know who the hell you are, and what kind of sick joke this is, but you certainly aren't welcome here."

In her ear laid flat to Daddy's chest, Yeo-deol heard the familiar erratic rhythm, *Dugun...Dugun...Dugun.* Yeo-deol did recognize this emotion from Dul's torments and growing pockets of darkness. *Daddy, why are you so scared?* The front door closed with a soft thud. Auntie had left. Immediately, Daddy's arms dropped out from under Yeo-deol, who clung on with her own strength. Daddy brought a hand up to his temple. Yeo-deol continued to hold onto him as her sisters dissipated back to their spaces. She finally let go into the inevitable fall to the ground once his heartbeat matched hers. Daddy retreated back to the place he had built for himself in his mind in Mama's absence.

A hush stretched over the air in the morning. Yeo-deol woke up feeling suffocated for breath. It felt like a deliberate labor to breathe through her nose as she pulled on her socks in the empty turret. Anxiety pressed into her chest as to what time it was. Net hadn't come to wake her up before breakfast as usual.

Running down the swirling stairway, Yeo-deol wished for the evening to come faster, like on each of the previous eight days. In the evening, all the maids emerged from their quarters to fill the hallways with gossip and exotic candies in their apron pockets. At the end of the hallway leading into the dining room, Yeo-deol saw her sisters clustered around the entrance without making a move to go inside. Yeo-deol's chest stung a little to have been forgotten. She shouldered her way into the dining room, ignoring her sisters' whispered protests and grunts.

There were messy platters of eggs and bacon on the table. No black coffee in the cups. "Good morning," Yeo-deol said calmly at the object of her sisters' fascination.

Auntie sat in a chair, wedged in at a corner of the table next to Mama's seat, drinking a steaming cup of water. Blankets were piled atop her shoulders, but her cheeks flushed at being acknowledged.

"Morning, Yeo-deol," Auntie said. She pronounced her name with Mama's ease, unlike the girls' Korean names that filled Daddy's mouth awkwardly. He suited the smoother, softer English words like his gray eyes and pale complexion. Unlike Mama who stumbled over r's and l's at times, though, Yeo-deol realized that Auntie also spoke the simple greeting with Daddy's ease in English. Auntie smiled bashfully with her entire face, her eyebrows crushed low over earnest eyes. Yeo-deol decided she liked that openness.

"If you don't mind, can you tell your sisters to come inside? They've been like that for a while now. I'm afraid I asked for a bit too much eggs and bacon this morning."

Yeo-deol heard the rustle of Daddy turning the page of his newspaper, carrying on his breakfast habit of reading as if the last eight days had not occurred. Yeo-deol picked up her fork and began to eat. After a few moments, the rest of the girls entered and filled in their seats. The girls ate the brittle bacon and yolk-wet eggs as slowly as they could, training their eyes on this mysterious figure, whose cheeks flushed deeper into the silent breakfast. Sleet fell outside, pelting off of the thick glass panes.

CHAPTER 3

Neither Daddy nor Auntie made a move to rise from the dining table as the maids reached between their elbows for empty plates. From the head of the table, Daddy's face was turned aside to the windows. Yeo-deol wriggled her toes as she drank her orange juice, the pulp tickling down her throat. Over the brim of her cup, she watched Auntie's eyes skip around and take in each girl. In the morning light, her eyes were more brown than hazel. They fixed momentarily on Yeo-deol's. Her pupils spun in the whites of her eyes like screws becoming rapidly undone. Yeo-deol coughed into her sleeve.

Leaning back, Auntie closed her eyes and brought her hand up to her temple. Daddy noticed this and with a nod to the maids lined at the wall, they swarmed around Auntie in overwrought tones of concern and floated out of the room with her swallowed up in their hive. Daddy stood up from his chair as well, rolling up the newspaper in his hands. He looked more like himself this morning, his smiling gray eyes crisp against a deep blue sweater. Daddy affectionately tapped down the row of heads and stopped at Il-gop.

"I want to hear your progress on the Vivaldi piece after lunch. No more playing around with Tchaikovsky," Daddy said.

Il-gop nodded meekly into her lap, but her gaze toward her sisters was fierce with a pride stripped away from their own. Yeo-deol felt the other girls shift in their seats. Across from her, Yeo-seot broke apart the bacon on her plate with her fork, slipping the greasy crumbs into her pocket for later when she was at her haunt over the record player, playing the music that Daddy adored.

In most regards, Il-gop was unremarkable at the violin, one year into taking up the instrument. She had no sense of rhythm, and Set, who was five years into learning the piano, often muttered that Il-gop made up entirely new songs from what was printed on the scores. Il-gop's greatest trait as a violinist, if anything, was her commitment to practice. She didn't play with the other girls, instead disappearing into the depths of the massive house with her violin and bow, only to emerge for meals.

"I tried to follow Il-gop to see if she was hiding something," Net had told Yeo-deol during a listless summer, "and I couldn't do it. The windows were open to let in the light, it was so bright and warm today, but then we crossed over this invisible line, between here and there. It was so cold suddenly, like something terrible was whispering into my lungs, and even the sunlight froze over us. One wrong breath, that's all it would take to shatter the standing light around us. I don't know how she can play music in such a place."

Yeo-deol tried to picture such a place of standing light and Net and Il-gop entrapped within the sheets of glass.

"No wonder she's so bad at the violin," Set had answered from behind, startling both Net and Yeo-deol.

Yet it was understood among the girls, including Il-gop herself, that she was Daddy's favored one, though he would never say so. Yeo-deol figured it might have to do with the fact that Il-gop looked the least Korean of the girls, with tawny hair lighter than Daddy's and a pink coloring that made the rest of the girls look sallow in comparison. Daddy unfailingly called her to his study weekly to listen to her play whatever piece she was working on, clapping along on his armchair with a firm hand. Except that too had halted since Mama went away.

Over the past eight days, Il-gop had gradually stopped going off alone to practice. She lounged around casually, digging her softened fingers into Yeo-deol's arm to tell her to fetch this or that. "You have to respect me," Il-gop said in response to any of Yeo-deol's complaints, their one-year difference stifling any of Yeo-deol's arguments with a look. Or it was Il-gop's generally impenetrable aura, more intense than Dul's hostility, that unnerved even the older girls into a wary agreeableness.

Before Daddy left the dining room, he bent over to kiss the littles. He gave a quick peck to Yeol, the youngest, before she could bite the tip of his nose. When he nudged his nose to Ahop's cheek, he nearly recoiled and exclaimed to no one in particular, "My God, how many days has it been since Ahop bathed? What do those giggling cows think I'm paying them to do?"

It had probably been more than eight days since Ahop was bathed. Somehow, Daddy had already forgotten how difficult it was to find Ahop, how Mama always insisted on bathing the younger girls herself, how she rolled up the sleeves of her dresses to lather their hair and tap down the length of their scalps in tickling songs. Daddy, after all, was leaving the girls to be herded by the cows.

Yeo-deol only belatedly remembered Ahop as she sniffed through her socks for a clean pair. *Clean, we have to clean Ahop.* Pulling Net along by the arm, they bounded down the hallway and rooms to lift silk curtains of various windows and check odd crevices for wherever Ahop had staggered off in her quiet way today.

"Oh," Yeo-deol heard Net breathe, "I found her!"

Following Net's voice, Yeo-deol ran into the gallery, not registering the room until her step faltered to a stop in front of the paintings mounted on the wall. The artists' names rolled off in Yeo-deol's ears in Daddy's matter-of-fact voice, names that weighed in Yeo-deol's mind: *Picasso, Monet, Van Gogh, Botticelli, Frida Kahlo.* The last artist was Mama's favorite, whose arched black brows kissed faintly in her solemn self-portraits. She dressed like Mama in bright dresses, and flowers and ribbons woven into her hair. Mama used to always stare intently at these portraits, as if trying to mirror back the solemnness, but Mama's eyes were too searing to match the artist's flat gaze.

In the middle of the wall of paintings hung four dust-laden tapestries, sent by Grandpa Henderson. Yeo-deol didn't like staring at the crudely-stitched scenes that were mismatched to the lushness of the surrounding paintings.

"Daddy, what are these pictures?"

A boat awash in an ocean reaching the ceiling. The contours of outstretched hands grasping fish and bread. A dinner scene of men numbering more than Yeo-deol and her sisters sitting at a long table. Thin rivulets of blood that ran down a waxen man's hands and feet, not enough blood for the expression in the man's upward-looking eyes.

"Biblical scenes, about someone else's divine love."

"Yeo-deol?" Yeo-deol startled at Net's touch. Her older sister looked concerned.

"I was telling you I found Ahop." Net pointed to Set's piano at the opposite end of the gallery, where sure enough, Ahop slept, pressed on the petals under the piano. Together, Yeo-deol and Net gingerly picked up Ahop and ran to the bathroom, trying to outrun their younger sister's odor.

In the porcelain tub, Yeo-deol and Net sat Ahop between them, wordlessly working out a system where

Yeo-deol massaged shampoo into Ahop's hair and Set shielded the half-open eyes from suds.

"Who knows when we'll find Ahop again," Net said, twisting the cap off the shampoo to dump a generous amount into Yeo-deol's hands.

The door handle began to shake.

"Occupied," Net yelled, lapping the lukewarm water running from the faucet around Ahop's stomach. The door handle continued to shake.

"Hey, I saw you guys run off with Ahop, and I kind of need her for an important decision," said Hana through the door.

"Not now," Net said with a growing edge to her voice.

But Hana wouldn't relent. The door handle shook over the stretch of silence as Yeo-deol rinsed out Ahop's shampoo, rubbing at missed spots that Net pointed out. When they finished bathing Ahop, Net stepped out of the tub in a slosh of water and slammed open the door.

"WHAT?"

Ahop's eyes drowsily opened to a stare, not totally dead to the world, it seemed. Afraid for the object of the brewing conflict, Yeo-deol lay her hand over Ahop's eyes and counted five slow seconds. *One. Two. Three. Four. Five.* When she took away her hand, Ahop had fallen back asleep.

At the doorway, Hana glared up at Net from the floor. She must have gotten caught in the force of the opening door. However, Hana had gotten what she wanted, and her face brightened as she entered the bathroom, not without a rough bump into Net's shoulder, to bend over the tub. Da-seot trailed in after Hana, blinking into the steam with an earnestness that softened the atmosphere. Inside the tub, Yeo-deol was uncomfortable at Hana's uncharacteristic interest in Ahop.

Before Yeo-deol could react, Hana picked up Ahop in a dripping swoop and scrutinized her from every angle, like the way the maids in the summer gardens held up watermelon to check for their ripeness. It felt like an exaggerated show the longer Hana dragged it out.

"Okay," Hana said, having reached a conclusion. "I'm going to official recast Ahop as Sleeping Beauty. I mean, look at the way she sleeps so naturally."

Yeo-deol exchanged a weary look with Net. It was the same pattern. Hana decided on a play to put on, and Da-seot eagerly accepted any role, small or big, because she idolized her oldest sister. Then Hana bullied Da-seot relentlessly because Da-seot was the prettiest. "She has the face I could have had, if my features had come together differently," Yeo-deol heard Hana say once.

The betrayal was fresh in Da-seot's pinched mouth, though she would forget this upset by the next day. Net's dimple appeared in her cheek. *Oh no.* Yeo-deol tried to signal at Net with her eyes, *it's not worth it, it's not worth it,* but Net straightened her spine and tucked her hair behind her ear.

"Yeah, but Da-seot's the *beautiful* one; the princess is called Sleeping *Beauty*, after all. She just has to close her eyes and she's the sleeping beauty. Meanwhile, you cast yourself perfectly—the witch who decides everything, the one who's twisted with jealousy," Net taunted.

Hana's right eye twitched, and a mechanical smile spread across her lips. She let go of Ahop in her hands.

Dugun...Dugun...Dugun. Yeo-deol's open mouth seemed to beat for all the room to hear, as Ahop dropped from Hana's standing height. In the airborne moment before Ahop landed into Yeo-deol's spread arms, Ahop's eyes popped open and clenched closed.

Dugun...Dugun...Dugun. Across Yeo-deol's chest, Ahop's body slackened back to sure sleep.

The base of Net's neck blotched to a pink color.

"Get out," she said.

Hana must have seen she pushed too far. She tried to discreetly peer into the tub on her toes to make sure that the whole of her ninth sister was, in fact, intact.

"Well, Da-seot and I need to practice her new role, so Ahop can rest until then," Hana said in a pitched tone, shouldering Da-seot out of the bathroom ahead of her.

"But all she does is rest," Yeo-deol heard Da-seot say in her sweet voice. A yelp sounded like that of an injured animal, and then there was silence. Net toweled off Ahop in the sink as Yeo-deol worked on draining the tub.

"Net?"

"Mmm?"

"There's something wrong with Ahop."

Net didn't answer. Nobody talked about it, even among the maids, how Ahop couldn't talk yet, how she could barely get through meals awake, how she ended up sleeping in such far corners of the house alone. There had been doctors who visited and talked with Mama and Daddy behind closed doors.

The only time Yeo-deol remembered seeing Mama visibly get upset was during one of Yeo-deol's last baths with the littles. Yeo-deol had sat with Yeol on the closed lid of the toilet seat, shaking out the beads of water on their legs. "Our own sleeping beauty," Mama had said with a laugh as she sponged Ahop, who was nodding off. Yeo-deol looked up when she heard Mama's laughter crumple into soft sobs. Mama gathered Ahop into her arms tightly. "Why are you so tired, my baby? What do you know about life already?" Ahop's face began to turn purple, but Yeo-deol didn't get to see anymore because Daddy had slipped into the bathroom, plucking Ahop out of Mama's arms. Yeo-deol was beckoned to wait outside the bathroom with Yeol, dripping in a window of light, as Daddy murmured to their inconsolable Mama inside.

Ahop was laid out on the circular bed next to the balcony on the third floor. Net had arranged paper flowers around Ahop's small body and veiled her sleep-bloated face in a pink, sheer cloth. Already, it seemed as if Ahop had been sleeping in this spot for many centuries. From the floor, Yeo-deol colored in hues of dripping egg yolks in her sketchbook. She was waiting for Net to come back from her usual rounds in the maid's quarters since it was the hour before lunch, when they left their rooms unlocked with potential treasures inside.

The blue pastel that Yeo-deol reached for dropped to the ground as her head was yanked backward. From upside down, Yeo-deol could only see Dul's black eyes. They faced each other forehead to forehead. In one hand, Dul held Yeo-deol's ponytail in a fist and in the other hand, she held an unopened box of cigarettes, probably a replacement for the one Set dropped out the window last night.

"For what you did to me last night, I could burn all these cigarettes on you until Daddy would throw up seeing you." Dul twisted Yeo-deol onto her back and pinned her in the stomach with one knee. She lit a single cigarette, cupping the flame to her face that Yeo-deol wanted to kick into her sister's face. Dul sucked in with the whole line of her jaw before expelling the smoke onto Yeo-deol's face.

"Yeo-deol, we need to breathe to live. I'll help you remember your gratitude."

Dul continued to smoke into Yeo-deol's face as Yeo-deol coughed and wiggled under her older sister's weight.

Dul talked over Yeo-deol, going through one cigarette after another.

"When I was grabbing the smokes, these maids were fooling around with each other on the veranda. That woman,

Auntie," Dul blanched at the word, "apparently sat outside in the snow all night long after Daddy refused to let her in. They all thought she had frozen to death, but she was blinking and rubbing her hands together. There were no footprints or tire tracks left, so nobody knows where she came from either."

Yeo-deol stopped resisting and let the smoke fall over her.

"Do you think she killed Mama?" Yeo-deol asked.

"Stupid," Dul said in a dull tone, shaking the ashes of her cigarette onto Yeo-deol's collarbone. "Mama can kill anyone she wants to."

"How do you know that?"

"It's not how I know it. It's just because you're too dumb to see anything."

With that, Dul eased off Yeo-deol. She swept the cigarette butts closer to the circumference of Yeo-deol's body to be cleaned up and rose to her full height to leave, satisfied with herself. But Yeo-deol was itching to know. She remained lying on the floor, afraid that any movement would set off her sister further.

"I'm not as dumb as you think. Tell me," Yeo-deol said, staring up at the ceiling.

"No, you wouldn't believe me. People call what they can't see with their own eyes a lie. I'm not a liar."

"Please, *unnie*."

Dul's ears turned red at the rare address for older sister in Korean, too sweet to be used between the two of them, but Yeo-deol really wanted to know. Dul sighed heavily. She stepped back to Yeo-deol, who intuitively tensed her body, but Dul simply sat against the wall, leaving a space for their mutual comfort. The usual taunting that lighted Dul's eyes and lips were gone. Dul crossed her arms over her knees as she seemed to consider something seriously in deep concentration. Finally, Dul's eyes settled on Yeo-deol.

Yeo-deol squeezed her eyes shut, her heart skipping a beat. She could already smell her singed skin in those perfect circles Dul liked to impress down her spine. Instead, Dul began talking.

"Don't say anything stupid to the others," Dul began softly. "But I know Mama's killed a man. She keeps him trapped in her telephone, the teal blue one we're not allowed to touch, and he calls at nighttime."

Yeo-deol craned her head up in alarm, but Dul lightly smacked Yeo-deol's forehead back down. To hear the rest, she would have to be absolutely still.

"On those nights, I wake up because the house turns really hot, and I'm so thirsty. I walk down the hallways for a long, long time because it's dark, until I reach Mama and Daddy's room.

"Mama is sitting on the bed with her back to me holding the telephone in her hands," Dul continued, "There's this terrible voice coming from it. He keeps saying how much he hurts, how far away she is from him, and it's so hot in the room that the skin on Mama's arms is bubbling and melting off."

Yeo-deol peeked up because Dul stopped. Real fear clouded her sister's pupils. Yeo-deol quickly put her head down, feeling as if she saw something she shouldn't have.

"I keep yelling at Mama to hang up the phone as my voice disappears, but she never turns around. We're each stuck in our individual suffering: the man in the phone, Mama's boiling body, and me, I just want some water. And for Mama to turn around and look at me."

Yeo-deol heard Dul standing up, but kept her eyes closed. She thought Dul had left the room when Dul said in a small voice, "One day, you'll grow out of drawing the world as you want to see it. Or I hope you do, or else you'll become blind."

In the silence, Yeo-deol stayed on the floor for another stretch of time to make sure that Dul had left for good. Groping around for the fallen pastel, she flipped open to a new page in her sketchbook, her eyes trained on the room already filling in before her mind. All she had to do was follow the lines with her hand: the blue and purple tones of the room Mama sat in, her melting yellow-toned skin, the shadow of Dul, and their teal telephone in Mama's lap.

FATHER

ALAN

1940

Alan Henderson was born for divine love, this he knew with certainty.

The smudged world in Alan's vision was testament to his special fate. For as long as Alan remembered, he had walked through a mist, stumbling unaware over peoples' feet. The borders of objects and structures materialized and peeled off in lines like cat whiskers. Gray blots of passing people were only identifiable by their outfits and voices.

His mother had feared for his eyesight, yet doctor after doctor concluded that twelve-year-old Alan, in fact, demonstrated perfect vision. It hadn't made sense for Alan in the hospital waiting room. He rubbed his eyes trying to clear away the invisible film that even the doctors couldn't detect.

A warm hand closed over Alan's hands.

"Sometimes son, there are unexplainable happenings." His father's smooth baritone tickled up the ends of Alan's earlobes. It was a voice that stirred awake the heavy-lidded eyes of the congregation to his homilies.

"I'm a freak. There's something wrong with me that the doctors can't see," Alan said, pulling the hands away from his face. Alan's father sat in a plastic chair next to him in his black priest outfit and white collar. To the surrounding people, it was an ordinary scene between a priest and distraught boy. If one looked closer, they might note their shared gray eyes.

"You're special," Alan's father said.

"Special?" Alan dubiously turned over his father's words. "I can read letters on a chart perfectly, but outside of here, I won't be able to see what's in front of me."

A deep hum reverberated from the throat of Alan's father in contemplation.

"I believe in God, Alan, and in that belief, everything and every happening has a purpose," his father said. Alan slumped into his chair; he didn't have much of an opinion on his father's God.

"Think of it like God is pressing His thumbs to your eyes so that someday in the future, He can reveal His divine love for you all the more spectacularly. This divine love will redeem and keep you. It will transcend your sin and the form of love as you know it to overflow with new life."

Alan's father smudged into the background as the words *divine love* captivated Alan's attention. His heart thrilled to imagine the film in his eyes falling away to reveal the crisp picture of divine love; there was no image for it yet, but Alan could taste the ghost of its fragrance: a sweetness that he couldn't place melted onto his tongue.

Alan looked up at the clicking sound of his mother's heels on the linoleum floor. The people in the waiting room also turned their heads as she passed. His mother had always been the most vivid person in Alan's smudged vision. Shifting spots of clarity over her figure pieced together to form the whole picture for Alan: her fine, white-blonde hair, pink cheeks, the sheen of her blue satin slip. She slipped a credit card back into her red clutch as she stopped in front of Alan, not acknowledging his father's presence.

Her calloused fingers gently lifted Alan's chin to look into the shock of blue eyes he didn't inherit. "I guess we'll listen to the damn doctors. Your beautiful eyes will be discerning enough," Alan's mother murmured, the souring warmth of her breath washing over him. The blessing was sealed with a kiss that momentarily brought a collective stop of breath in the room.

Music was Alan's first love, inextricably connected to his mother. As a violinist, his mother had quietly risen in the San Francisco Symphony and flew to different cities spaced out between the seasons to play with different symphonies. Alan had never watched his mother play in person. She was very private about her music. The click of the lock from the second floor, which was entirely her practice space, indicated that she would be absent for several hours, often for the whole day.

At these times, Alan listened for an identifiable passage, picking through the vinyl records once the composer or movement came to mind. This way he could match what his mother played upstairs in isolation. With an ear pressed to the horn of the record player, Alan loved how the bloom of music in the air cast everything in a pure sensibility. The swelling notes would anchor the lines and colors of his surroundings for the duration of the piece.

At age thirteen, Alan told his mother that he wanted to learn the violin.

They had been lounging in the brightly illuminated courtyard, their shoes kicked off on the white pebbles. In Mama's hand, she swirled a flute of champagne and by her closed eyes, had been probably working her way through a recital in her head. She lowered her sunglasses and gave him an uneven smile at his announcement.

"Why?" his mother asked.

The question pricked at Alan. He had expected his mother to be happy.

"Music makes the world settle around me. What if the violin is the divine love that I've been missing out on because it's always been too close?" Alan answered. He could already feel it in his fingers. His eyes would clear up. He and his mother, they would play for the finest audiences dressed in the amber hues of wines that his father bought as gifts for his mother.

While his mother didn't understand Alan's talk of divine love, she relented to his desire to learn the violin. "Anything for you, baby," she said, pulling him into her arms.

Alan entered at last through the locked door of the second floor, which turned out to be nothing like what he envisioned of sunlight and light breeze, and worn wooden floors on which his mother napped. He was struck by the coldness of the space. The whole expanse of the floor was encircled by mirrored walls and closed off from natural light except for a window of skylight in the middle of the room. A single music stand was set up directly beneath the skylight.

The practices were grueling. As a violin teacher, Alan's mother was clinical and precise, completely divorced from her usual soft-spoken glamour. She paced around him, using a white baton to tap at his hand over the fingerboard.

"No, no, no, it's all wrong," she said, loosening his curved fingers to correct his grip.

Eventually, Alan would lower his violin in frustration as the room began to blur over his mother's empty soothing, "You're just beginning, this is natural for everyone." He was not like everyone else, though. He was special, born for divine love.

The last practice ended with Alan's violin crashing onto the floor. The gray blots that had been growing in the mirror and darkening over the weeks surged around Alan and swallowed him up in blackness.

"I can't see!" yelled Alan, doubling over on his knees, rapidly blinking to no avail. His mother's panicked fingers fluttered down his arms and neck. Later in the evening, the darkness receded as Alan lay on his mother's lap with a bag of ice over his face. His mother had been right. The violin was wrong for him, and he had known since entering the second floor. He would recognize his divine love when he encountered it with his discerning eyes, as his mother said.

Alan's mother was trying to talk discreetly on the phone, as if Alan's temporary blindness had somehow rendered him deaf as well. "… you mean you can't drop by? I'm telling you, our son was practically possessed by the devil himself. Hello? Hello? *Fuck*, Ted." Her voice cracked over his father's name.

The violin lessons stopped without any further discussion. Alan dragged the record player up to his bedroom on the third floor and went back to listening to his classical records, though there was no more attempts to match to his mother. He played whatever fit his mood, Brahms, Dvořák, Mozart, Vivaldi.

1952

For a time, Alan willfully forgot about his fate of divine love because of two women.

It ended badly both times.

A twenty-year-old Alan jumped from the third-floor balcony overlooking the courtyard after his first girlfriend broke up with him. The screech of violin jarred in his ears as his body hit the pavement. Laboring from his wet breaths, Alan clasped his hands together with excruciating effort and pictured the devastation of his girlfriend upon hearing the news. He smiled. She would come in his favorite dress of hers, a baby blue cotton that peaked her tiny nipples and the ridges of her collarbone, and climb into the casket with him to burn to ashes together.

In his fading vision, his mother was at the end of the tunnel, thrashing his body in rough shakes with the fragile fingers he had not been allowed to hold as a child. Her cries were unmusical and ugly, something he found a final comfort in, more than his father, who had come home for the night and, faced with his son's death, wavered through the Lord's Prayer.

Alan did not die, to his disappointment. He instead spent six months in a hospital room, during which his ex-girlfriend never visited. His mother became his fixed bedside guardian. She would stare at him sullenly, swilling sips of vodka between her teeth from a water bottle, her bare face looking nothing like his mother who gazed at him under her pink-hued eyelids with such love. He closed his eyes.

Four years later, Alan was sure he had met the woman he would marry.

"Are you sure about this, Alan? You're still so young to marry," his father said. He wore plainclothes for their rare family dinner at this seafood restaurant, far out of the way of his parish. In the following pause of what his father left unsaid, Alan sensed the more essential reason: *She's too old for you to be marrying her.*

The woman was twenty years older than Alan. In fact, she was the same age as Alan's mother, who looked tired and much older in the dim candlelight, tugging at the neck of her gray sweater in agitation. His mother had stopped wearing her vibrant gowns that dipped under her delicate shoulder blades. Alan had come home two years ago from college to find his mother sitting on the white pebbles of their court-yard with her dresses piled around her. "None of them will zip up," she had whispered.

"We love each other more than anything," Alan said, filling in the silence. He ran his thumb across the gold band he had slipped on the woman's finger as she napped beside him earlier in the day.

They were celebrating nothing, in a night of leaving things unsaid. His mother had been dismissed from the San Francisco Symphony after twenty-four years; the seasonal concerts playing with different orchestras had long dried up. "They like 'em young and fresh," his mother had said dismissively when she broke the news to Alan alone first. Alan suspected it may have had more to do with her constant drinking, carried around in bottles that fooled no one.

Alan let his mother crack the lobster shells open for him with her tremoring hands. Since the fall, Alan had lost some strength from his fingers and legs, although the doctors had claimed a full recovery.

Crack crack crack crack.

His father raised his eyebrows at Alan and the woman and sighed before picking up his wine glass in a toast of concession. Alan laughed and squeezed the woman's thigh at the seeming approval. Her eyes skittered from him to his father nervously. She pulled her hand out of Alan's grip to drink from her wine glass in rapid gulps, her other hand drumming the table top.

A week later, the woman escaped him.

"You suffocate me," she exhaled, dropping the gold ring into his hand. The woman got up from the diner booth with a flutter of a twenty dollar bill. Alan sat in the diner, finishing his coffee, which wet his stomach and curled back up in his throat. He walked past his car in the parking lot with this choke, looping his car key ring around his index finger. His feet led him for a half hour past fields of orange trees, the road he had driven down so often in his childhood, until he stopped in front of his father's rectory. The front door had been left open a gap.

Alan entered into the familiar threshold. A familiar shirt was flung onto the shoe rack. Shaking his head with a laugh, Alan picked up the shirt and proceeded upstairs, gradually picking up his girlfriend's entire outfit. So when Alan opened the door to his father's study, he wasn't surprised to see his father and his girlfriend's naked bodies contorted into one other on the desk. The hard lines along the bookshelves knocked into Alan, stunning him in a pain that cleared his smudged vision momentarily. They were ugly. They didn't even look human with their clenched eyes and shrilling cries. He left the woman's folded clothes by the door.

The sun blazed just over the horizon by the time Alan arrived back home. His mother had fallen asleep at the long dining table, probably waiting up for him. Alan threw out the half-drunken glass of champagne at her hand and sat blankly next to her. He continued sitting there until a faint knock sounded on the front door.

Alan opened the door to the woman.

"Why are you here?"

"I owe you an explanation."

Alan turned back inside the house, not caring if she followed him in. He sat down at the dining table again, next to his mother. The woman sat in the chair across from him.

"I hurt you, and for that, I'm going to be punished," the woman began with a conviction he could not argue against. She enunciated each word calmly on the lips he had so surely traced as his a matter of days ago.

"Why did you do this to me, then?" The question sounded pathetic even to Alan's own ears. He was born for divine love, yet here he was, deprecated to a fool's betrayal before his own eyes. The unbelievable cliché that his girlfriend had been fucking his father behind his back.

The woman ran a hand through her gray-streaked hair.

"Everybody told me I was crazy for dating a boy twenty years younger than me. That I was asking for trouble. I did it anyway because I loved your passion, your *youthful* passion, that always urged toward something great and already looked beyond me and this moment."

Loved.

"But?" Alan pushed.

"But it was like I told you, you suffocated me. You looked too far beyond me, you began to pin on me your notions of greatness as if they were mine. I have no excuse, but I forced you to see what you refused to see."

What he *refused* to see? The woman couldn't have known how mocking the words were, but Alan climbed up onto the table to hold her throat. It was slim and pale, easy to crush for any other stupid noise she made. Had she always buzzed with this much noise? The woman watched him peacefully as her face took on a purple pallor. He realized she was subjecting herself to her own punishment rather than him subjecting her to any recess of shame. Alan dropped his hands. The woman slumped forward briefly, breathing softly, and then stood up to leave, clutching her throat.

I am better than this, Alan told himself.

Tomorrow, he would enlist and go somewhere far, far away from here.

CHAPTER 4

———

Yeo-deol couldn't hear or see or feel. She tried to count her shuddering breaths. *One, two...two...What came after two?* Turning her head with great effort, Yeo-deol squinted at a blurred form that solidified into an outstretched hand. Her upturned fingers twitched in the blood coming from her own body. *So this is the color of blood,* Yeo-deol thought. Past her hand, her sisters' kicking feet came into clarity. They were closed around Dul, whose open mouth only showed through their ankles, taut around a soundless pain.

Dul had been the first one to reach Yeo-deol sprawled out on the paved stones. Dul had also been the one to push Yeo-deol off the balcony. Yeo-deol's eyelids fluttered into parts of the day that swam in her darkening consciousness.

At breakfast, Auntie sitting in Mama's seat, the wedged-in chair from the previous breakfast, appropriately signaling her outsider status, gone. She must have seen how darkly the girls' faces clouded over because she startled out of the chair, running a hand through her hair. Then Daddy's solid command to Auntie: "Stay."

Guarding the door as Net picked through the maids' jewelry. "They shouldn't be able to have prettier things than us," Net had said in a bright tone set behind a smile that weighed in Yeo-deol's stomach.

Helping Da-seot draw lines around her mouth for her new role as the princess's mother. "Hana told me to not move or even breathe if I can help it," Da-seot said, puffing out her cheeks in demonstration. "The queen sleeps forever with jeweled tears on her cheeks. Even at the end, it doesn't matter if she wakes up or not because everyone only cares for the princess."

Pounding on Yeo-seot's back, bowed over and throwing up into the toilet bowel. Between heaves of air, she cried for the emptiness that would start over again in the pit of her stomach.

Gathering Net's hair into her hands to braid in thin ribbons of white satin. They sat on the circular bed on the third floor, talking seriously about Auntie and where she must be in the house at that very moment. As Yeo-deol listened to Net's theory—"She must have found the place where Daddy keeps all our money, and that's why he's letting her stay"—her gaze kept straying to the wall where Dul made her confession the previous day. Like a summoning, Dul flew into the room, her long black hair lashing behind her, and gripped Yeo-deol by her armpits before Net could react. They stumbled onto the balcony.

"What did I tell you? Don't say anything stupid," Dul said, backing Yeo-deol against the rail overlooking the back of the estate.

"I-I didn't say anything."

"You're right, our little artist doesn't need words when you can draw Daddy a picture. How could you draw the room and give it to him like some sick gift? That room's mine. Daddy may have given you compliments, but he called for me separately."

Dul pushed her face into Yeo-deol, who clenched her eyes closed at the menacing proximity.

"I'm sorry," Yeo-deol said meekly.

"He said I was deluded, that I should start seeing doctors for my 'night terrors.' He asked me, how could Mama be talking to some other man?"

Something in Dul's tone made Yeo-deol open her eyes. She saw her terror reflected back in Dul's widened eyes.

"I know it was real. Do you know how many times I died in that room?" Dul touched the base of her throat. "My whole throat dried up and my tongue fell out. I couldn't stick it back in no matter how much I tried, this shriveled, ugly thing."

Yeo-deol screamed as Dul dipped her over the rail at the waist. Dul bent down to lift Yeo-deol up by the ankles, so that she hung suspended upside down in the air. All Dul had to do was let go, but even as Yeo-deol's head grew heavy with the rush of blood, she thought her sister wouldn't. Or she wanted to believe Dul couldn't do it as proof of a remote love beneath the cruelty and tortures.

Dul's face appeared in the gap between Yeo-deol's bare feet.

"Die. Die just once for me, and you can see the room with me next time."

Terror worked up Yeo-deol's throat, gagging her wild sounds into a silent plummet to the ground. Yeo-deol steeled her eyes to the downward rush of the pavement coming to meet her.

Yeo-deol woke up submerged in water lapping under her ears. Only her face showed through the surface of the water. She couldn't move her body, but every breath bristled with the shards of her shattered bones swirling through her body. The air was warm, and the sky above her was a shade of teal blue that she had never seen before. Yeo-deol had somehow left the winter.

Without Daddy or her sisters to mark time, Yeo-deol remained lying in the water as the red sun bled away into a lavender night. Yeo-deol felt safe. She had no fear, no desire, as the tide slowly pushed her closer to shore until her cheek brushed against a familiar pair of faded brown shoes bound to the earth by thin blue roots. Yeo-deol reached out to touch the soles of the shoes and then took her hand back, confused at the impossible ease of her body. Sitting up carefully, Yeo-deol marveled at the stiff newness of her bones that had hewn together in the time she spent in the water.

As Yeo-deol crawled further up the shore, her eyes tracked up over the shoes and length of the long legs that were connected to Daddy, who was leaned up against a wide-set tree of a burgundy color. The blue roots to which the tree darkened into split in the middle, suggestive of splayed legs. Daddy's eyes were covered by his hands like he was crying, an image that reverberated in Yeo-deol's chest with wrongness.

"Daddy, wake up," Yeo-deol whispered. She pressed her ear against Daddy's chest as she had done the night Auntie arrived. Although she heard a faint pulsing, it was buried faraway from where she was. Yeo-deol hovered a hand to his nostrils that stirred with the slightest breath.

"Daddy," Yeo-deol repeated. Daddy was close to the dark. If Yeo-deol split open his chest right now, he would run with the darkness that was missing from this soft night. But no body should ever have to hold in itself what belonged outside it. Yeo-deol looked up at the burgundy tree to the orange globes that hung from the sparse green leaves. It seemed to be an orange tree. Yeo-deol tried to scale up the tree for a branch to cut open Daddy with, but she kept sliding off.

"I'm only trying to make Daddy better," Yeo-deol said, smacking the unyielding tree.

Yeo-deol knelt to the sloping ground, glaring up at the tree as she cradled the splinters embedded in her hand. At this angle, she saw how the branches of the tree bent and warped under the weight of its oranges. There were ten oranges of different sizes and hues, just enough for her and her sisters. Scooting back on her feet, Yeo-deol took in the tree's pathetic shape that coiled into itself. She felt bad for the tree. From beside Yeo-deol, Daddy's hands were still fastened over his eyes, but his cheeks glistened. Perhaps what Daddy needed wasn't emptying out the darkness but rather being filled with something bright and of substance like the oranges. And Yeo-deol could help unburden the tree of its oppressive oranges.

When Yeo-deol put her hand up to the tree's trunk again, it warmed under her hand as if it understood her intentions. "Please," Yeo-deol implored the tree as she slipped her gown over her head and tied the arms around her waist. With a step onto Daddy's shoulders, Yeo-deol climbed up the tree easily this time and carefully crawled across the different levels of branches to pluck each orange into the lap of her skirt that she held up by the corners.

Just as her hand curved around the last orange, Yeo-deol lost her footing and slipped into a fall through the tickling branches, the soft night, the sweetened water, and then the last stop of pavement that clapped upon Yeo-dol's cheekbone.

Dark eyes crowded Yeo-deol's view. Humid air curved onto her stomach oppressively.

"She's awake, call for Daddy!" one of her sisters yelled. A dull pain followed down Yeo-deol's bound arms and legs as the room behind her sisters came into focus. She didn't recognize the room. The massive bed Yeo-deol lay on was decorated in a canopy of pink lace that knotted around the posts, matching the curtains. Strings of tinfoil stars hung down from the sparse wrought-iron chandelier above their heads. A wooden piano sat in the corner, different from the sleek black one that Set practiced on.

The drenched material of Yeo-deol's gown stuck to her skin as she shifted her shoulders in discomfort. Daddy burst through the door. When he saw Yeo-deol through the cluster of her sisters, Daddy lowered his head in an exhale before walking more calmly to the bed. Yeo-deol's eyes fixed on his brown shoes, the same ones he wore under the orange tree. Her throat loosened as Daddy sat beside her and tipped his forehead against hers. She touched his plain cheek and cupped her hands to his eyes as she remembered. Had her fall from the tree woken him?

"How long have you been sleeping, Daddy?" Yeo-deol asked. She dropped her hands to look into Daddy's eyes that anxiously circled around her. He began to answer, but her sisters' laughter edged in and obscured what he said.

"Do you think she'll be dumb now?" Yeo-deol heard Il-gop ask. Yeo-deol clenched her teeth, taking in her sisters' clenched lips and amused eyes. In moments like this, she hated her sisters the most, who knew exactly how to reduce one another's suffering to nothing, believing their individual suffering was the greatest. Twisting her features in an exaggerated grimace, Yeo-deol brought her hand up to her temple as Auntie had done. Daddy gripped her hands tightly.

"What's wrong?" Daddy asked.

Yeo-deol averted her eyes from her sisters. "They're making me dizzy, make them leave."

The room buzzed with shrieks of protest as her sisters were ushered out of the room by maids. Net's gaze burned into Yeo-deol most of all from the exiting procession, and Yeo-deol faltered in doubt. Maybe not all her sisters had been laughing with Il-gop. Yeo-deol waited for the sound of the door closing before she looked back up to Daddy.

"How did you wake up?" Yeo-deol tried again, raising her eyebrows meaningfully. Whatever meaning was lost as Daddy shook with laughter into their clasped hands, but his laughter was genuine and softened by the bewilderment in his roaming eyes.

"Funny child, that's what I should be asking you. I've been awake three whole days—that's how long you've been sleeping."

A bead of sweat ran down Yeo-deol cheek. Time had always been a constant thing for Yeo-deol, passing strictly on the face of a clock, but everything seemed so blurred now.

"Is it already summer, Daddy? I'm so hot."

"I'll tell the maids to turn down the heat." Daddy leaned in against her damp forehead, a private gesture that he only did with Mama when they thought the girls weren't looking. "Don't leave me like that again. Each and every one of you is Mama to me. I love you all so much, it hurts me."

No, Daddy, I'm Yeo-deol. But Yeo-deol didn't want to hurt her Daddy anymore, so she let him smother her in a hug as he cried into the dip of her collarbone. Yeo-deol's face continued to drip with sweat. In that way, they both cried together for a while.

Yeo-deol was left to recover apart from her sisters in the pink room, named for the light it would take on through the curtains. According to the other girls, it was far from their glass turret in a wing of the house they had never entered before. For the first time, Yeo-deol slept alone and she began to grow irate. Unlike the glass turret, the walls enclosed the windows of the room, boxing Yeo-deol inside the house totally. She missed the endless view of the glass turret, and the feeling of holding a pastel in her hand, nonetheless the ability to hold anything in her hands while her arms and legs were bound in stiff casts.

The only breaks in Yeo-deol's moods were when Daddy came to sit at her bedside in the evening for an hour or so. He drew what Yeo-deol wanted in her sketchbooks. Flush at her closeness with Daddy, Yeo-deol would hand him colors silently as his clumsy hand scrawled out pink elephants and bowed over petunias, feeling as if the warmth in her chest would pour out and drown the room. During one of Daddy's visits, he had looked around the room.

"This is the room your Mama stayed in when she was pregnant with each of you girls. I wasn't even allowed in here." Yeo-deol sank into the sheets and breathed deeply for any lingering remnant of Mama, knowing she had been the last one to touch them.

Her sisters came by during the day with offerings: little pots of paint to decorate her cast in unimpressive pictures, and thin slices of differently colored cakes from Mama's pantry that didn't quite taste right. None of the girls mentioned Auntie, and Yeo-deol didn't ask. She was too tired.

In an assembly of all the girls except for Dul and Ahop, Hana adorned a pink string around Yeo-deol's neck with the pantry key. "After almost dying, I think Yeo-deol has earned the right to be the keeper of Mama's pantry," Hana said with a hard squeeze on Yeo-deol's shoulder.

Yeo-deol saw the way Yeo-seot's hands nervously turned together, and the quiet way Yeo-seot's eyes fell. Even Il-gop's lips twitched, though she hadn't outwardly competed for Hana's affections to win Mama's pastries. Yeo-deol could have refused or done the more noble thing of giving the key to Yeo-seot, who needed it the most by how her face had seemingly hollowed out since Mama went away. But Yeo-deol limply nodded.

The girls filed out of the room, all but Set who remained sitting at the wooden piano where she had been observing the ceremony. Yeo-deol sat in silence, not knowing what to say. Set was generally detached from the girls and held a serenity that the girls respected, different from Il-gop's unapproach-ability. Yeo-deol didn't know if she had ever talked to Set alone. However, that didn't seem to be Set's intention because she wordlessly rose from her seat and left too.

Later that night, Yeo-deol wasn't surprised to open her eyes and find Set standing over her bed. Yeo-deol let herself be lifted into a wheelchair, procured from she didn't know where. Set pushed Yeo-deol down the hallway lit by the full moon in the upper windowpanes, taking sharp turns and squeezing into what seemed to be impossible spaces before they entered them. They stopped at a metal door, and on a panel with two arrows, Set pressed the lower one.

Ding.

Set slid open the metal door and a metal grating that folded out after it. It was an elevator, in their house. Yeo-deol was stunned as she was wheeled inside and Set closed both layers of the door. Set turned a lever to the left, and the car began to move downward, based on the passing levels.

"We have an elevator in the house?"

"There's a lot of things we don't know about the house," Set said. She looked over to Yeo-deol and knelt down so their eyes were level. "Hana dumped the pantry key on you because since you'll be on crutches for a while, it'll be months, maybe years if you forget, until you would check the pantry."

Ding.

Set went through the same motions of opening the two layers of doors. They walked in total darkness for a time, the wheels occasionally catching on something indiscernible, until they finally emerged into the familiar hallway of the dining room and ballroom. Set kept going until they reached the kitchen. The air was fragrant with the cream soup that

Yeo-deol had eaten off a tray hours before. Huge vats were tipped upside down on the metal table, and a mount on the wall glinted with ten knives, from smallest to largest.

Set reached behind a clustering of dried spices that hung from the ceiling to the floor. Without looking at Yeo-deol, Set's hand gestured for the key. Yeo-deol quickly leaned in with the key still around her neck, impatient to see. The lock in the wall clicked open. Set pulled back the wheelchair to open the door, and they both looked in. It was empty inside. Yeo-deol blinked, trying to will the beautiful cakes and jars of cookies from her memory.

"Daddy may have not known when he handed over the key to us, but Mama stopped baking months ago."

Yeo-deol ran her fingers along the shelves that were gathering dust.

"Why did she stop baking?" Yeo-deol asked.

"She ran out of rat poison. That's why she didn't let us eat anything from here."

Yeo-deol had no idea what Set was talking about. Mama's pastries were beloved by Daddy's friends.

"I knew the pantry was empty; Dul too. If Hana hadn't known when she first took the key, that greedy little thing knew by the time she started making a competition out of it."

"You knew all along."

Set shrugged. "How could Dul or I break it to any of you when it made you so happy? It was twisted, but we were willing to go along with it, at least until today."

The word *we* held in the air on the unspoken topic of Dul's absence since Yeo-deol woke up.

"What have I been eating, then?" Yeo-deol asked as her stomach dropped from beneath her. All the colored slices of cake that Yeo-deol had eaten, the hard-won tarts she had seen Da-seot or Yeo-seot tenderly eat with mussed up hair, what had Hana been feeding them?

Set laughed. "Nothing bad. Hana's not that smart. Those desserts from the maids that all of you turn your nose at because it's not Mama's—she stashes away part of it and then messes up the remaining ones so they look unappetizing. None of the maids can say anything. The cake slices you savored this week? They were the same ones you refused to eat last week. You taste what you want to taste."

Yeo-deol stared at a spot of crumbs as Set wheeled her out of the curtain of herbs. She thought of the chocolate cookies she had eaten with Mama the last night before she went away. Had Mama poisoned those too? They proceeded back to the elevator in the same unrelenting darkness, but Yeo-deol didn't pay much attention. Back in the pink room, Set helped Yeo-deol get back into bed.

"Why did you tell me this, if I could have never known?" Yeo-deol asked. Set tightly tucked in the blankets under Yeo-deol's chin so that it strained across her neck.

"I wanted to give you a real prize after almost dying," Set's voice wavered.

CHAPTER 5

——

Low murmuring and giggles slipped over Yeo-deol in the pale morning. Her body was soaked in sweat, confined to the rigid outline that Set had tucked her into after their trip to Mama's pantry. The stiff casts bound over her left arm, length of her waist, and right ankle burned with heat, stifled beneath the plaster. The room had grown hot throughout the night, as if someone was slowly turning up the temperature in the house to begin a fire. *Was Dul going to the room with Mama and her telephone?* Resigned to sleeplessness, Yeo-deol had tried to block out the darkness of the room that swarmed under her ears and nostrils. She trained her eyes on the tinfoil stars hanging from the chandelier.

Eleven stars, she counted, eleven for the girls and Mama, maybe.

In this room Mama had spent personal time with each of the girls before they were born. Yeo-deol could picture Mama drifting past her to play a familiar lullaby at the wooden piano in the corner, and then her hand reaching into Yeo-deol's view to caress each tinfoil star. It felt like Mama had created this room specially for the girls. In this comforting sweep of images, the dark of the night gave away to a less dark dusk.

"That's the thing about winter, it just goes from dark to less dark, and less dark back to dark," Mama had whispered the previous winter with her forehead pressed up against the chilled glass. Yeo-deol had looked out, confused, to the winter day outside, and before her other sisters could cover her mouth, she said, "What do you mean, Mama? It's still light outside." Mama rubbed at her eyes before bending down to hug Yeo-deol. "That's right, like can see like," she had said against Yeo-deol's shoulder, "so it's good that you see the light." The likes and lights had swept through Yeo-deol's head incoherently.

That had been a difficult winter, when Mama would often go back to bed after seeing the girls had eaten the breakfast she prepared. But she had been better by spring, and that's what all the girls counted on this winter as well, from wherever Mama had gone away to.

Yeo-deol angled her head toward the person at the door. The man's back was turned away from Yeo-deol; he was in conversation with the flustered maids in the corridor, but Yeo-deol recognized the faded brown bowler hat and dark beaver fur coat. He used to visit Mama during the difficult winter.

"Ah, my little patient seems to be awake. If you'll excuse me, ladies."

More giggles fluttered around the room until the door closed. The man leisurely took off his coat and hat and hung them at a mounted rack by the door. When he turned around, Yeo-deol's throat squeezed with the need for a pencil to map out his appearance. Blond wavy hair, like the angels inside the girls' illustrated Bibles and on the ballroom tapestries, and shameless blue eyes that surely had swallowed a bit of the sky. His massive nose, sharp and not unlike a bird beak, and thin-lipped smile clashed with the angelic features, yet altogether it was a strange combination that pleased Yeo-deol the closer he got to her.

"Hello, you must be Yeo-deol," the man said, pulling a chair to the bedside. "I'm Dr. Roberts. How are you feeling?"

"Fine, thank you," Yeo-deol muttered without much thought, though she was still trapped under the blankets. Dr. Roberts raised his eyebrow, taking in her sweat-soaked hair and the stiff angle of her chin cramped with the sheets.

"I guess somebody didn't want you to get away and accidentally fall from the balcony again," the doctor noted in a wry tone that colored the word, *accidentally*, in a way that stung at Yeo-deol's eyes. Daddy must have told the doctor that she had fallen alone, by her own stupidity, and the doctor didn't believe him. Yeo-deol felt the blanket loosening under Dr. Roberts's patient hands. He folded the blanket back to the corner of the bed, allowing cool air to ease over Yeo-deol's body.

"Thank you," Yeo-deol said.

"Of all the things to be thankful for," Dr. Roberts muttered over his briefcase bag.

Yeo-deol felt her cheeks warm in embarrassment at the vague reprimand. She averted her eyes toward the door that had opened a gap, through which her sisters' hands groped the air to stroke the sleek fur of the doctor's coat. Dr. Roberts followed Yeo-deol's gaze and swiftly got up to close the door with a definitive click of the lock. It was as if he clicked something locked between the two of them, and fear sifted in Yeo-deol's stomach.

The doors were generally left unlocked in the house without question, except for when Daddy and his friends gathered in the study. Yeo-deol hated that particular locked door around which Hana and the middles gathered to admire the pretty turn of cigarette smoke coiling out from the bottom. Sometimes playful fingers drummed through the crack to catch the girls' hands, and Yeo-deol uneasily watched her sisters' mouths gape open in muted delight. Nothing good came out from locked doors.

"Okay, shall we begin?" Dr. Roberts had settled back into his seat with an open notebook and a scarlet fountain pen rimmed in gold balanced in his hand. She saw him writing the familiar letters of her name, her own page in this notebook.

"Do you know how many days it's been since you've woken up?" Dr. Roberts asked.

Yeo-deol shook her head. "Not since I counted past my fingers."

"Good, good," Dr. Roberts talked as his pen moved in a furl of mesmerizing script, "You have a good sense of time if you're trying to count. It's been about two weeks since you woke up. I'm sorry I couldn't get here to see you sooner, but there was heavy snow in these parts of the woods."

The doctor went through a series of checks, prodding and lifting her arms and legs in different directions. All Yeo-deol had to do was lie still and tell him if the pain got to be too much.

"You've healed remarkably fast for the extent of your injuries," he said with a chuckle. "I guess nothing beats being young. The bruising should let up in a few days."

Yeo-deol wondered if a grown-up like him would believe in the sweetened waters that had hewn her bones back together rather than his materials of plaster and bandages.

As Dr. Roberts made some notes in his notebook, Yeo-deol's eyes roamed over him, the texture of his curls and the slight line of his mouth that somehow contained the booming voice sinking richly into her ears. This was the closest Yeo-deol had been to a grown-up man other than Daddy and his friends, and Daddy's friends were more shadow than human. Net had laughed at Yeo-deol's description of Daddy's friends: "If they're shadows, how can we see them?" Yeo-deol repeated Mama's words from the difficult winter: "Like can see like."

Dr. Roberts closed his notebook and leaned forward with his hands tightly clasped together.

"Two weeks ago, when we were first applying the plaster on your broken limbs, it came to my attention that you have quite a—" Dr. Roberts's lips twitched to find the words, "collection of scars on your back, in a very neat line." The doctor's *very* was mincing; he already seemed to have formed his conclusion.

"They looked like cigarette marks," Dr. Roberts added. He paused in what he was going to say next, staring down at the fountain pen in his hands.

"Yeo-deol, do you need help?"

Each word in the question stacked onto Yeo-deol's lungs, heavy with implication.

Yeo-deol's mind reeled for an answer. Whatever she would tell him, he would take it with him when he left the house and the woods, and the truth felt like cutting off one of her fingers, though which finger it was she didn't know yet.

"I'm fine, thank you," Yeo-deol said, repeating the phrase she had been taught to reply with to adults. And that was largely true. Dul's anger was not a regular occurrence, and Yeo-deol could usually avoid it by sticking to her other sisters, who weren't subject to Dul's brutality.

The dotting of cigarette burns the doctor saw were from a dinner party before the snow and before Mama disappeared, when the trees had deepened to auburn. Daddy's friends had sat at the long dining table extended with additional tables in an endless stretch. Yeo-deol crawled beneath the table, fascinated by the array of shoes, and bumped into Dul, whose cheeks and eyes had burned as she grabbed Yeo-deol.

The doctor continued to twist the pen in his hands, clearly not convinced. His eyes leisurely flickered up to Yeo-deol, willing to wait for a better answer.

"Mama and Daddy don't know about it. It's not their fault," Yeo-deol blurted because that was the most important truth.

The skin around Dr. Roberts's eyes pinched as if he was trying to scrutinize her confession in the air. They sat in this ruminative silence as the morning light from the window faded away. Snow was beginning to fall outside. Yeo-deol licked the beads of blood she drew on her chapped lip. The last thing Yeo-deol wanted right now was for Dr. Roberts to end up getting snowed in and continue asking her questions to which even Mama and Daddy didn't know the answers.

Something lightly skimmed Yeo-deol's cheek, pulling her out of her worries. Dr. Roberts pointed the tip of his scarlet fountain pen to her. "I hear you're a budding artist. A gift for you. It uses the finest Chinese ink, where your Mama comes from."

Korean, Mama's Korean, Yeo-deol thought without correcting him since he was an adult. It was all the same to men like Dr. Roberts. Yeo-deol began to turn away, but the doctor's next words caught her and made her tremor: "In fact, the ink is so potent that it's illegal in the US. You see, it can kill a grown man within an hour of entering the bloodstream."

Dr. Roberts closed Yeo-deol's fingers around the pen.

"I'm really fine," Yeo-deol started, but panic closed up her throat at the end of the sentence. Her body was deadened to her desire to shake off his hand. She didn't want the pen in her possession. Art wasn't supposed to be a terrible weapon. Yeo-deol tried to be honest in her drawings and sketches to the world and emotion around her, that which she couldn't comprehend yet. Dr. Roberts's blue eyes looked down on her with pity.

"I'm not asking for anything. It's a gift."

With that, Dr. Roberts left with the promise he would be back in two weeks to take off her casts. Yeo-deol stared at the falling snow in the window as the feminine giggles in the hallway started again. The maids no doubt were surrounding the doctor to stroke his blond hair and marvel at his eyes. Yeo-deol took comfort in imagining that they ignored his ugly nose and lips—that's how the maids would describe them, *ugly*, for a lack of better words. As snow piled up steadily on the sill, Yeo-deol tried to fill in the gray space of the sky with what the doctor had written on her page of his notebook. *A missing mother, her ten shadows, and a lying father.*

The days slipped by under a layer of fresh snow that muted the noise of the house. Or it may have had more to do with the halting of her sisters' visits, the novelty of Yeo-deol's near-death having worn off. The evenings with Daddy stopped too. Even Net went from sitting with Yeo-deol breakfast to dinner, to coming by only to drop off more brushes and paper that accumulated unused on a dresser. Dul had yet to show her face, neither did Set come back after her bewildering reveal of Mama's emptied pantry. Yeo-deol couldn't be sure now if she had dreamt it. The only evidence was a faint *ding* that sounded in her ears at odd times and bounced around her head.

Although Yeo-deol's bruises had lightened to a yellow-green shade as Dr. Roberts had said they would, Yeo-deol didn't have the willpower to pick up a pencil or pastel. She stared at the offensive fountain pen that was nearly buried under reams of textured paper. Instead, in the time Yeo-deol spent alone, she had taken to drawing scenes and images in her mind. The picture didn't form immediately. Yeo-deol had to focus for long periods of time in order to bring out the exact detail and shades of color, her eyes fixed to the lace canopy above her as her vision receded around her.

The most vivid scene she had formed in her mind was of a miniature Set pulling the lever in the elevator. Yeo-deol formed the tight line of her sister's nose and expressionless lips, and the mild gaze looking into the passing floors. Just as Yeo-deol grasped the image fully, the elevator would plummet, dropping Set into the darkness wherever Dul must have been. The two of them, Dul and Set, were tied to each another in a closeness that was more intense than the natural groupings within the other girls. "They're twins that happened to be born separately," Mama had once said to soothe the girls' bitterness.

Sometimes, the ringing grew clear and more rapid, as if coming from directly inside the curve of Yeo-deol's ear. *Ding. Ding. Ding. Ding.* The scene that formed, beyond Yeo-deol's control, was in the elevator again, but instead of Set, Auntie stood alone. The ends of her hair curled under her ears, remarkably grown out from the shorn hair of not so long ago. Most egregious, though, was the dress she wore that was surely Mama's, a black skirt overlaid by a stitching of red flowers that seemed to have blossomed on her skin. She worked the lever with frustration, stopping the elevator on every floor with hungry eyes. She was looking for something.

On a morning scrubbed of clouds, Net finally seemed to miss Yeo-deol's company enough to come visit. The uninhibited sun washed the room in an airy pink that seemed to have been cut out from a more beautiful past. Yeo-deol lingered in this half asleep until a gentle knocking pulled her out of the picture she was working on in her mind. In the doorway, Net stood warmly smiling, holding a bundle wrapped in what looked like one of the littles' blankets, and in her other arm, Yeol bared her teeth in greeting with the rumblings of a growl. More like a dog than a girl, Net had apparently braved their youngest sister's vicious bites in the time she spent apart from Yeo-deol.

"I know you're mad at me," Net said, "but I don't think you'll be mad much longer once you see what I brought you."

Yeo-deol's curiosity was stronger than her bitterness, and she watched eagerly as Net untied the bundle on the bed. There were new pots of paint on which Net had scribbled out the owner's name, a bushel of wet flowers, and a box of chocolates. The chocolates were the prize of Net's most recent sweep of the maids' quarters.

"They're called vod-ka chocolates," Net said, flourishing the lid off the pin-striped hat box set on Yeo-deol's lap. "It was under the one redheaded maid's bed. I figured she probably won't miss it."

The bed gradually became smeared with paint as Yeo-deol painted paper flowers, and Net nimbly braided the real flowers into wilting crowns with her slender fingers. Net held up a fresh flower to Yeol's nose. "Flo-wer," Net pronounced for her sister, who either didn't know how to speak yet, or chose not to speak. Yeol ate the flower, biting down hard enough on the skin between Net's thumb and forefinger to draw blood. Net laughed and sucked at her thumb, scattering flowers around Yeol with her uninjured hand to do as she liked, accustomed to the behavior by now. Yeo-deol noted all of this warily, wondering how much she had missed out on being apart from the other girls.

"I haven't seen Dul since she pushed me off the balcony," Yeo-deol said, stating the plain fact that had been tugging at her in the past weeks.

Net popped another Russian chocolate into Yeo-deol's mouth. Yeo-deol winced at the burst of bitter liquid she bit down on. She had lost track of the number of chocolates she had eaten, but it felt as if her emptied mind had become unrooted from her head to hang among the tinfoil stars above.

"We're punishing Dul," Net said with a shrug of her shoulders. "Who knows which one of us she'll want to kill next? Daddy knows who's been taking his cigarettes all along now too. He was so mad that he didn't look mad anymore."

Yeo-deol nodded, chilled at the collective *we* that was defending her, that maybe it hadn't all been for show the night Auntie arrived and her sisters gathered around her closer than they ever had. *Auntie, what had happened to Auntie?* Yeo-deol tried to will the elevator scene of Auntie in her bleary state, but she couldn't recall any concrete details of what Auntie looked like, much less the dress that Yeo-deol had pored over for over hours picturing. All that remained was knowing that Auntie had been wearing Mama's dress and looking for something desperately.

"What about *her*?"

"What about her?"

Yeo-deol blinked in confusion at Net's indifferent deflection of her question. She felt Net's hand on her forehead, easing Yeo-deol down to the pillows that were much more plush than she remembered them.

"I think I may have overfed you the chocolate." Net's voice funneled over Yeo-deol's head like folds of melting taffy as she faded away into sleep. Net talked about Auntie.

"She's been gone since the day you fell off the balcony. Her and Daddy ran out from his study together, and by the way she reacted seeing you on the ground, you would have thought she saw her own body. She turned around and ran into the woods with this terrible screaming. No one could follow her because the snow was knee-deep. She plowed through all of that, that's how spooked she was.

"The maids were chaos around Daddy, asking him for the doctor's phone number, where they should move you, if they should make arrangements with a funeral parlor just in case. But everyone stopped talking because Daddy's face was becoming purple. We all thought he might have died standing up. But then he began yelling so loudly that it shook the trees.

"I couldn't tell if he was upset about your fall or Auntie running off. Why did they come out of the study together? Not even Mama was allowed in there.

"But the eeriest thing is I sneaked into the room that Auntie had been staying in, while everyone else clamored at the front of the house for the doctor to arrive. I wanted the green sweater, the one she wore when she first showed up. But I couldn't find it anywhere, and the clothes she'd been borrowing were folded up all nice and neat on the bed. When I sniffed at the pile though, the clothes smelled exactly like Mama.

"And I thought what if she had actually been Mama? Same but different enough to feel wrong. She was right under our noses and we missed her, Yeo-deol, just like that, except it may be forever this time."

CHAPTER 6

———

"I'm back!"

Dr. Roberts's cheerful voice called from behind Yeo-deol, who could only twist her head so far in her position. He had returned as promised. Moments prior, the maids had flurried into the pink room to flip Yeo-deol onto her stomach without explanation. Yeo-deol had squirmed against their silent conspiracy, the pain of her movements seething between her gritted teeth. "Get off me, get off of me, you dirty cows."

Dr. Roberts dropped down in his chair in the periphery of Yeo-deol's vision. He held down the top of his felt hat with one hand, as if it would blow away in the breezeless room.

"The poor maids. How are you already so vicious with your words?" But the doctor was laughing in a way that lightened Yeo-deol's mood too. Even in his laugher, his keen gaze studied her intently like last time, so different from Daddy, who was always turned toward something else. Yeo-deol turned back the bed's headboard, discomfited at what else he might record in his notebook about her.

"Do you remember why I'm here today?" Dr. Roberts asked.

"Because you promised," Yeo-deol said.

"I see you hold up promises very seriously," the doctor said with a chuckle, "Though isn't it quite meaningless if you don't care for the reason behind it?"

Yeo-deol's chest burned at yet another offhand rebuke. Dul had thrown her off the balcony for breaking an implicit promise. Dr. Roberts had no right to judge her vicious way of speaking when his words insinuated and implicated, rooting into Yeo-deol like seeds to become truth.

"Come on, don't be angry with me. I was speaking generally."

"I'm not mad."

"I can see your bottom lip jutting out."

Yeo-deol inched her bottom lip in. The mattress dipped under Dr. Roberts, who leaned against the headboard to face Yeo-deol. His white shirt was unbuttoned at the top, showing a grotesque tangle of dark hair that didn't match his blond curls. Yeo-deol's eyes tracked upward to Dr. Roberts's hand that remained planted over the felt hat.

"You've been healing remarkably well, especially given that I haven't been able to visit with you as much as I'd like.

Congratulations, you get your hard casts off today!" Dr. Roberts lifted his felt hat to reveal pink earmuffs over his blond curls.

"A congratulatory gift," he said, slipping off the pink earmuffs to put them on over Yeo-deol's. She tried to glare at him, but the flush starting in her cheeks probably gave away her pleasure. His previous, more terrible, gift was shut into the far corner of the squat dresser between them, where Yeo-deol planned to leave it.

A muted whir filled the room.

Dr. Roberts held up an electrical saw in his hand, the spin of the circular blade glinting in the light. "Ready?" he mouthed. Yeo-deol raised her uninjured arm to the earmuffs, realizing they had not been some gift of whimsy.

Still, he hadn't needed to get her pink ones.

Yeo-deol nodded in reply, and Dr. Roberts lowered the saw onto the hard plaster enclosing her waist. In a clean line, he sliced through the plaster with a steady hand, followed by the cool nudge of scissors cutting along the padding under-neath. An odor rose from Yeo-deol's bared stomach, but Dr. Roberts's face didn't shift as he leaned in to cut through the casts on her wrist and ankle. Yeo-deol waited for the flinch, for the inevitable cut into her skin. It never came.

There was one place in Yeo-deol's mind as her crutches tapped down the hallway. She ached to see the sky and the natural light of the glass turret. The pink of Mama's nursery room had lost its charm over the weeks of Yeo-deol's growing solitude. Meanwhile, the glass turret became like a memory, a conjuring of a secret place in her imagination. How could she and her sisters sleep every night in such a lovely place?

Yeo-deol halted in her step at the click of a maid locking the pink room behind her. Her stomach gave a twinge of unease, but she didn't look back. Aware of the maids' presence, Yeo-deol heaved exaggeratedly and ran her right hand down the length of her dress, as if to wipe her sweaty palm. Once Yeo-deol covertly confirmed the faint outline of the fountain pen, she resumed following the maids ahead of her through the unfamiliar wing of the house. Yeo-deol had chosen to take the pen last-minute, leaving the pink ear muffs inside the dresser as a replacement offering—it hadn't sat right with Yeo-deol to take both.

The walls of the hallway were painted a soft orange that endowed a summer lull even though the windows framed a definite winter scene of endless white banks leading nowhere. As Yeo-deol continued walking, the walls deepened into a deep ochre that passed into the nondescript cream color most familiar to Yeo-deol as she reached the main staircase. Her sisters' voices echoed closely from their individual spaces. The maids that had led Yeo-deol ahead of the way were already gone, diverted into the kitchen to prepare for dinner.

Yeo-deol labored up the stairs using the crutches to pull herself up some ten steps. Each step up lurched with the possibility of falling. Objectively, the distance between the step Yeo-deol climbed up to and the ground floor was harmless compared to the plummet she had survived from the balcony. Yeo-deol was certain, though, that she would die this time; the sheer terror of the fall would stop her heart before her body hit anything.

Exhausted by the death that looped in her imagination, Yeo-deol sank down on the next step and secured her crutches between the rails of the stairs. Reaching up with her uninjured hand and the lift of her foot, Yeo-deol crawled up the spiraling stairs.

She needed to confirm that the glass turret existed, that there was more to the sky than the boxed-in view of the windows in the pink room. The light dimmed in the passing windows as Yeo-deol drew nearer to the glass bottom of the turret at the peak of the stairs.

It felt momentous when Yeo-deol opened the blue door of the turret with a faint hand and collapsed into a thick blanket discarded near the entrance, probably Hana's. Hana tended to wake up while walking to the door, the blanket slipping away from her shoulders when she turned around, alert and brimming with a new day of ideas.

Snow was piled atop the glass domed ceiling, muffling the room in shadow. Yeo-deol's sigh puffed in the air. At the sound, the bunched up blankets next to Yeo-deol stirred. *Ahop?* Yeo-deol wondered as she reached inside the blanket and touched velvet, maybe one of her sisters' dresses. Her hand felt across the expanse of a forehead too broad to be any of the littles.

Dugun…Dugun…Dugun. Yeo-deol quickly tried to pull away, but her arm was locked beneath the blanket.

"If you kill me, the other sisters are going to torture you in more ways than you ever did to me," Yeo-deol tremored.

Dul's dark eyes glared up from a slit in the folds of the blanket.

"I can do worse things to you without killing you."

The threat sat in the air. Yeo-deol knew that she was essentially trapped in the glass turret unknown to Daddy, her sisters, or even the maids. Yet something resembling anger more than fear rang in Yeo-deol's ears as she brought her free hand down over Dul's eyes with a resounding *thwack*. There was silence. Yeo-deol stared at the palm of her hand, not certain if one was allowed to slap a person in the eyes.

"You can be upset with me since I tried to kill you, but don't think the other girls are any better. They knew all along what I was doing to you, yet they waited until I pushed you off the balcony before making a show of protecting you."

Yeo-deol curved her hands into tight fists, trying to will back the touching memory of the parade of her sisters, Set tucking her into bed, Daddy bent over her sketchbook with his tongue peeking through his lips in concentration. Dul hadn't been there to see any of it.

"You didn't even come visit me after you tried to kill me," Yeo-deol said, trying to clamp down the hurt in her voice.

"The others didn't let me," Dul said. She hadn't made a move to emerge from the covers.

Yeo-deol paused and slowly uncovered the blanket. *Dugun...Dugun...Dugun.* Dul's turned face didn't diminish the devastating sight. The long black hair that used to sweep over Yeo-deol was gone. Dul's ears jutted out, looking over-sized on her shaved head.

"Who did this to you?" Yeo-deol asked, unable to fathom such violence. It felt like Yeo-deol was seeing her sister naked.

"I won't apologize. I really did want you to die," Dul said softly, as if she hadn't heard Yeo-deol's question. Yeo-deol considered the meaning behind Dul's words.

"Does that mean you don't want me to die anymore?"

Dul looked at Yeo-deol with her black eyes.

"If I kill you, I'll become trapped in the phone inside Mama's room forever."

"You don't want to kill me anymore because you want to preserve your own life?"

Yeo-deol blinked at her sister's selfishness.

"There's nothing to preserve," Dul spat. "It was either you or me falling off the balcony that day, and I pushed you." Dul spoke as if there had been a greater force orchestrating her actions. She had a wild, almost insane look to her wid-ened eyes and the spit gathering in the corners of her moving lips. This was not Yeo-deol's cruel sister.

"Something's wrong," Dul continued. "Mama is gone, and the man's voice is silent inside the room. All of you are there sitting at a long table that has replaced Mama's bed, and

I'm trapped inside the phone. I ring and ring from inside it, and I know you're all there. But none of you answer."

Yeo-deol stared down at her sister, who couldn't kill her now no matter how much she wanted to. Without much thought, she reached down to pinch Dul's nose between her thumb and index finger.

"Tell me you're sorry, and the next time I'll answer the phone," Yeo-deol said. Dul's face took on a blue pallor, yet she refused to degrade herself by opening her mouth.

"Say it." Yeo-deol could feel the weight of Dr. Roberts's fountain pen in her pocket. The turret grew darker, as if the toxic ink was already flowing out and leaching into the snow packed around them. Hairline fractures started to form in the surrounding glass. Beneath Yeo-deol's hand, Dul's black pupils tensed, threatening to crack open and leak thickly into the room.

Yeo-deol released Dul, whether it was out of fear of the turret falling apart or her older sister's eyes cracking open. Dul flopped into the cushion of blankets. There was a stop in everything as Yeo-deol uncovered the blanket over her sister's chest. Upon seeing the faint rise and fall, Yeo-deol let out a wail that should have shattered the turret. *I'm no better than Dul or my sisters.* From below them, a smattering of feet pounded up the stairs, growing closer. Yeo-deol tried to stop her tears as the door banged open. Net ran in first and pulled Yeo-deol up by her tender wrist. *Ah,* Yeo-deol exhaled sharply. The entrance of her other sisters filled Yeo-deol's breath. *Too many, too many of us in one place.*

"Daddy, she's been here all along," Net said to Daddy, who had stopped at the threshold of the door, taking in the circular room of the glass turret.

Yeo-deol couldn't remember if he had ever been inside the turret. She wished that this wasn't his first view, that he could see the sky and the expansive view of the estate behind the snow. Daddy stepped past Hana, Set, Da-seot, Yeo-seot, and Il-gop, who followed him with their eyes. He knelt in front of the pile of blankets until Dul sat up.

"Dr. Roberts waited for you for two hours," Daddy said. He didn't seem to be fazed by Dul's shaved head. His eyes were trained on Dul like they were the only ones in the room, waiting to hook her eyes into obedience.

"I told you, I don't want to see him. He scares me," Dul said, not meeting Daddy's eyes. Her back curved outward, as if she was stomaching all her shame at once.

Yeo-deol wriggled in Net's arms, listening closely at the revelation that Dul had been seeing Dr. Roberts too. Dul didn't have any bandages or visible injuries like Yeo-deol, though. *I haven't been able to visit with you as much as I'd like*, Yeo-deol remembered Dr. Roberts saying earlier in the day. She wondered if she was imagining the regret now, if he also gave Dul gifts.

"Can't you see, Daddy? Dul was trying to kill Yeo-deol again. What'll keep her from hurting the rest of us?" Net said, enunciating her words with spite. This suggestion had an effect on the other girls, who seemed to shift away from where Dul was without moving their feet. Only Set remained still, her blank gaze directed at the floor.

Yeo-deol was becoming uneasy. She could see that Net had taken her near-death personally. The outspoken condemnation of Dul in front of Daddy frightened Yeo-deol, going entirely against Net's usual stealth in which she slipped through rooms and could drive the maids mad one at a time as they never found what they needed.

"Dr. Roberts could probably turn around and stay for dinner. It hasn't been so long since he left," Daddy was saying.

Dul put her head down on her knees. "Don't pretend like you or Dr. Roberts want to help me. I'll kill myself first before either of you can, before any of you can."

Yeo-deol again couldn't understand what was going on, the word *kill* sticking to the middle of her forehead. But before Dul could resume what she was saying, Net heaved Yeo-deol up by the armpits into a standing position.

"I'm going to help Yeo-deol downstairs with the other girls. I don't think it's safe to be around Dul."

Yeo-deol felt herself being dragged away from Daddy and Dul. They stopped at the door, where Net seemed to have one last thing to say: "We used to have that white, fluffy dog, remember, Daddy? Her name was Marble, because Mama got it confused with 'Mabel.' And we had to eventually get rid of Marble because she wasn't safe to be around, right?"

Daddy paled at the thinly-veiled implication. Dul didn't react, but the devastation of hearing Net's words landed on her shoulders by the slightest drop, a drop that only Yeo-deol saw. Yeo-deol's chest ached. If she allowed herself to be dragged out of the room right now, Yeo-deol had a feeling she might never see Dul again, that Dul would be stuffed into the telephone inside the room, and Yeo-deol wouldn't be able to hear her ringing.

With a yank of her shoulder, Yeo-deol pulled herself free from Net, who stumbled back in surprise. Yeo-deol crashed to the ground in a fresh wave of pain. As her sisters closed in around Yeo-deol in concern, she swatted away their hands.

"Don't take Dul away," Yeo-deol bawled, her fingers blindly wriggling toward Dul. She was no better than Dul, and none of the girls were better than the other. They suffocated one another by their sheer number and were cemented in their individual alliances, but it was wrong to pick out and get rid of only one of them for what they collectively formed.

A lack of words, a lack of coherence, a lack of air bore down oppressively in the turret.

The dinner bell rang from downstairs, *ring ring ring,* each chime stirring the girls and Daddy out of the stupor of Yeo-deol's meltdown. Net had already disappeared from the turret.

As Daddy carried Yeo-deol down the twisting stairs, she tugged at his ear.

"Daddy, what did Dul mean, all the things about you and the doctor?"

Her vision shook as Daddy jostled her slumping body.

"It was nothing. Merely delusions of grandeur and paranoia," Daddy answered in a roll of big words that left no room for other questions. Yeo-deol touched the veins that popped out in his neck.

"Are you going to listen to Net and take Dul away from us?"

Daddy didn't answer.

"If each and every one of us is Mama to you, you can't do that," Yeo-deol insisted, throwing back the exact speech that had moved her so deeply when she woke up.

Air breezed through Yeo-deol's ears as Daddy lifted her up, so as to look her in the face.

"I can, but I won't," Daddy said with a smile. His gray eyes were leached of light in the darkness of the stairwell, following the natural rules of shadow and light that Yeo-deol knew from sketching. Yet a picture began to take form in Yeo-deol's mind as Daddy lowered her and continued down the stairs: the heels of Mama's green shoes sticking out from a plot of frozen soil, the rest of Mama submerged beneath the earth, her eyes closed and blood dried on her forehead. Daddy's empty eyes looked down on the green heels. *I did because I could.*

FATHER

ALAN

—

1961

Alan told himself he was not the kind of brute who reveled in war. He couldn't even call it "war" precisely, this suspended state of affairs he had merely existed in for nine years in Korea. When Alan had enlisted, he envisioned a quick death in combat, which his mother saw through immediately. "Don't throw your entire life away for one person," she had said.

Like you did for Father?

He had been disappointed to arrive in Korea and learn that the hostilities had already melted into halting negotiations by then. Yet Alan stayed. He stayed even after the fighting officially ended, building up an unremarkable career doing administrative and clerical work. There were worse places Alan could be in, worse things he could be doing, as the constant refrain of his mother's letters reminded him: "What if they transfer you to Vietnam?"

Still, seeing the other GIs playing house with Korean girls, girls in every essence of the word, felt like a form of violence. It was sick, mad really, but the men were all going mad here with vague boredom and the definite sense that they weren't wanted here. On the streets, they loomed over the black-haired heads, averting their gazes from the people who so obviously hated what they stood for in their uniforms. The peoples' eyes here had a liquid depth that burned through Alan's fogged eyes; they resembled tears on individual faces, but clustered in crowds, they became a deeper, coiled rage that could unravel upon itself for an eternity with just one tug.

It was more comfortable for Alan to keep to the base, and even then, he couldn't avoid the girls who visited and sometimes turned to Alan with their brightly hued lips. "I baby," one girl had said to him, holding onto his arm, "sexy baby." He shook her off, panicked at the rounded aspect of her cheeks and her child-sized hand.

Alan wrote letters to the woman over the years, gradually filling up nine cookie tins, all different variations of an apology he couldn't seem to get right. Alan had to perfect the letter that would allow him to return to the US again.

In the most recent, he wrote: *Dear, living here in this foreign country over these long years without you has made me breathe in new air. I think I understand what you meant*

by my suffocating you. I am suffocated here in these peoples'
eyes, they look at me with eyes that are so sad yet vicious—it
is as if they want to undo my whole being, and every day I
have lived is in resistance to that. Is that how you felt? Please
understand that whatever suffocated you, it was ultimately
rooted in love and the belief that together, we could become
greater than our individual selves. I still believe that you love
me more than my father, and I have learned from my pun-
ishment. You still love me, don't you, dear? One word is all I
need, and I will fall back into your lap in utter devotion. I can
accept this blurred world if you are in the center of it, if you
are the one to lift me up and save me.

In his first year in Korea, Alan had thought he was going blind.
The quality of the blindness, though, was different than the first
assault of darkness he had experienced once as a child. It was
as if a tunnel closed around his vision, and through the middle
he could see the papers he transcribed on the sleek typewriter
furnished by the army, and the hands that he turned over and
over again to confirm that they were indeed connected to his
body. Everything else was pitched in a darkness disoriented
by the noise of men's chatter and the stench of perfumes and
oil-drenched foods brought onto the base.

The darkness only made sense in a recurring dream.
Alan was a child again, sitting at a table, and it was his birthday. "Baby, make a wish," his mother said into his ear, her
unrelenting arms around his throat. Not wanting to hurt

his mother's feelings, Alan mustered all the energy he could exert into leaning forward to the candles, until it felt as if his neck muscles would pop. This agonizing physical effort was marked in time by Alan's mother adding one more candle for each passing year, until Alan's adult legs reached the ground.

When the candles finally warmed on his lips, an inch more and they would singe, Alan drew in all the breath in his lungs and blew out the flame. A perfect darkness would descend in that moment, blanketing Alan in a smooth cloak of peace he had never known. His mother gone and his body disintegrated in a light breeze, the remaining darkness was left with the echoes of nameless compositions wavering in vibrato.

In Alan's waking moments, the other men avoided him, and Alan didn't particularly begrudge them. "Word from the bird is that if you look into Henderson's eyes, there's nothing in them. Look directly into them and *bam*, it's like he can see through you," Alan overheard someone whisper during a birthday party, Alan's twenty-fifth, that had been held more as an obligatory gesture to the unsociable soldier.

"Yep, down to your red polka dot boxers," Alan answered in a deadpan before continuing to flip through the menu. That small moment of stifled laughter was enough to disarm the wariness around Alan, at least to Lester, the whisperer from the birthday party.

"No hard feelings, right?" Lester asked in a way of introduction the day after the party. Alan looked up from his Spam and cheese sandwich and grunted, "Sure."

Lester took an unexplainable liking to Alan and began to seek him out regularly for company. Part of the medical department, Lester spent most of the day in a separate building, but they sat together during meals and piled their laundry together on Sunday nights. Lester filled up the conversation effortlessly, not relying on a back-and-forth. Through the inane chatter, Alan learned Lester's life story. Born and raised in Texas, Lester had enlisted at the tender age of eighteen, days after marrying his high school sweetheart. She sent carefully typed letters in lavender envelopes, which Lester made a show of passing around to the other guys. "You smell the vanilla? She's sweet down to her pores."

Alan refused Lester's constant invitations to visit the club, always the same three words of fresh hope: "How about tonight?" Alan went as far as the curb to see Lester and the other men off in their cabs. Better were the mild nights when Lester stayed in and would eventually show up, knocking on Alan's bunk with a pack of cigarettes. "Nothing like a smoke under the bare ass of the night," Lester crooned exaggeratedly, shaking his blond curls in laughter. Some of the other quiet guys joined them outside with six-packs of Budweiser and Coca-Cola in silence. In this easy company, Alan's strange blindness let up to the familiar smudges, assured by Lester's solid hand that steered Alan away from the assault of reality and the knocking clarity of seeing his mother in his friend's blue eyes.

"You're hitting the ten-year mark, Henderson."

Lester took a sip of the black coffee Alan set out for him. His eyes widened slightly and coughing, he pushed the cup across the table to Alan.

"Almost ten years, and you can barely make some decent coffee?"

"That's what a wife is for," Alan said distractedly. The beginning of a new letter was taking form in his head. *Dear...* He had a feeling this would be the one. He would send this letter and return to the US.

Ripping off a page on the calendar pinned to the wall, Alan stared at the bold one announcing the first day of December. Indeed, thirty more days and Alan would be celebrating his tenth year in Korea into the new year.

He and Lester sat over breakfast in their shared condo. Their friendship had evolved into the likes of a well-worn domestic partnership over the years. They took turns shopping for groceries weekly, though Alan was always shouldered out of the kitchen by Lester. In the summer when it was too hot to sleep in their beds, the two of them sprawled out on a blanket in front of the open balcony door with chilled cans of beer between them. "Where's your husband?" the guys called out cheerfully when one of them was spotted without the other.

Alan turned back to the table at Lester, whose mouth had frozen in a mild smile. It was the same mild smile he wore five years ago, when instead of a lavender envelope, a manila envelope had arrived containing signed divorced papers. Lester's wife had tired of waiting in a long-distance marriage for a husband who expressed no interest in returning home.

"You know I didn't mean—"

"It's good, man. I just get dumb in the head sometimes when I hear that word. Like I imagine her, I *smell* her vanilla perfume, and I want to bash her head in until she becomes dumb like me. Make her feel the way she made me feel. Isn't that what love is, reciprocity?"

Lester leaned across the table to take back his coffee. Alan tried not to stare at the pink slashes working up Lester's neck, the drag of someone's fingernails. Even while living together, they maintained their individual privacy. Lester didn't acknowledge the cookie tins that lined the window sills, even after Alan had come home to find Lester casually eating the cookies from their wrapping. Alan also didn't question what Lester spent his time doing outside of the condo, sometimes for several days at a time, at the second apartment he was making payments on.

Seeing how deflated Lester looked, resigned to his rancid cup of coffee and the bitterness of his failed marriage, Alan's pity stirred him to say the words that Lester had long given up on.

"We could celebrate my almost ten years. How about tonight?" Alan said the three words slowly, meaningfully.

Lester's eyes brightened in recognition, plucked out of his dejection so immediately that Alan wondered if he had been putting on an act for this exact moment.

"Almost ten years later and Henderson's finally letting me show him the *real* Korea," Lester hollered, nearly tripping out of his chair.

The real Korea. Alan mulled over this throughout the day, the suggestion that he had been existing inside some false Korea that would fall apart like a theater set. Some of the guys clapped his back in conspiratorial tones of see you later's. Lester had spread the word, and it became apparent a full-fledged party was in order. Alan felt a bit embarrassed, considering he still had thirty days for the actual reason of celebration.

Back in the condo in the evening, Alan didn't have much to prepare after showering and buttoning up the new shirt his mother had sent in the guise of his father. An ambiguous gray clustered around him, several other guys who had gathered at their place to ride in a cab together.

Sitting on the couch, Alan adjusted his wire-rim glasses and line of vision to not see the smudge of the girl who waited for Lester at the doorway. Her black head swayed as she shuffled here and there in her white heels to avoid the men's shoulders, making a tiny yelp whenever someone reached under her miniskirt to pinch her butt cheek.

Lester emerged from his room, looping an arm around the girl's waist. He threw his head back, his blond curls bouncing, and hollered, "Let's gooooooo."

The "real Korea" was a bar, or some kind of club. Over the pulsing music and thick air of sweat, Alan ordered a glass of orange juice and sat at a table with the men, who had already forgotten him for the women squeezed into the booth with them. Hands caressed his cheeks and lingered down his arms, female hands, and their voices babbled at him in nonsensical English.

Alan's head lowered against the dizzying, faceless clamor around him. A touch lighted on his chest softly. Alan breathed in a potent suggestion of rose and the keen edge of something else from the hand. With a tentative reach, he held the resting hand and turned it over to sniff, thinking back to the bottles of perfume on his mother's dresser. None of them smelled like this. The woman giggled. "So you can smell it? It's soybean paste. *Deng-jang*."

Alan couldn't hide his surprise at the fluidity of her English.

"I was hungry earlier today, but I was so sick of burgers and steaks. I just wanted rice and some stew, damn!"

The woman took a sip from his glass.

"Are you from the US too?" Alan asked, wondering if someone's girlfriend from home was visiting, despite the near impossibility of her joining them in a club like this.

"You're funny. Do I have to wipe off my makeup for you to see me? You big Americans are so dumb, but funny."

Alan drained the rest of his juice and let the woman lead him back farther in the back of the club until the noise no longer reached them. The door shut, and he heard her hum as she quietly took her clothes off. Alan walked backward into what was definitely a bed. Kicking off his shoes, Alan laid on his back and blinked as the woman climbed atop him, unbuttoned his shirt, and discarded it to whatever floor held them up.

A few hours or minutes later, Alan opened his eyes to a dim orange light and the woman's bare backside. Sitting up with a hand to his temple, Alan's breath strained as he looked down at the thin cotton sheets bunched up around his waist, and the cramped room that was dominated by a dresser piled with stuffed animals. For the first time, the gray blots had cleared away, and his uninhibited vision vacillated in the clarity of colors and textures.

In excitement, Alan touched the woman's back, wanting to hear her exclaim "Damn!" when he shared the news. "I told you getting laid is a cure for everything except death," he could hear Lester saying.

The woman's back shook. Alarmed, Alan turned her around by her shoulders to see that she was crying behind her hands.

"One more time?" she asked, uncovering her face. Seeing his face seemed to loosen her cries into the air.

Alan backed off the bed to the floor. Although her features were still slightly blurred, the shape of her face and the big, dark eyes that stared back at him were distinctive of a child, a mismatch to her full breasts he had suckled at blissfully. She had long black hair and the liquid eyes that stared back at him on the streets. She was a Korean girl. Alan closed his eyes to shut out the image that was forming before him.

"How old are you?" Alan asked calmly.

The girl paused to gather the sheets around him, understanding that he was done.

"I'm supposed to be six ten," she said, stumbling over the number. The girl's big, dark eyes stared at him, the clearest feature in Alan's vision.

"Sixteen," Alan said to himself, "sixteen."

"Sixteen," the girl repeated back, thinking he was correcting her English.

Alan stood up to leave, his chest weighing with a guilt he felt he didn't deserve. He hadn't known better. The girl jumped off the bed and blocked the door with her outstretched arms.

"You have to pay," she said.

A sharp crack sounded in the room from Alan's chest. Or maybe it was the girl's head that hit the wooden dresser as Alan pushed her aside, suddenly needing to get out of the tiny room. Alan ran past the few people dancing on the floor and his table where the remaining men slept with their faces buried into the nooks of Korean girls' necks. Alan ran outside and fell to his knees in a vomit of orange juice that burned up his throat.

Alan lay heaving on the wet street as his vision clouded. The lines slipped off the tops of buildings, and the luminescent street signs and people speaking over him disappeared behind a gray mist. Had it been a momentary grasping of divine love that cleared his eyes? The childhood haunting smarted in Alan's chest. *No, no, no, divine love can't come in a prostitute.* Laughter bubbled out of Alan's mouth at such ludicrousness as he felt himself being lifted up.

The familiar dream recurred in the night. Alan blew out the candles. His mother, however, gathered up the cloak of perfect darkness in her arms. "It's not yours to have anymore," she said in a fierce hiss, as if she knew what he had done, and Alan was left alone in her absence, a blinding white that erased him grain by grain.

Lester's worried eyes bore down on Alan when he came to consciousness.

"I'm not exaggerating when I say it sounded like you were being dragged through hell and back. I was ready to call the chaplain to perform an exorcism," Lester said.

Alan raised his hands to his wet cheeks.

"No more club nights." Alan's voice was hoarse.

"Definitely not," Lester said dryly. "My husband can't even handle orange juice, apparently."

Despite Lester's recommendation to rest for the day, Alan went to work. The remaining twenty-nine days stretched before him unbearably, and Alan wanted to be occupied. At his desk, Alan pushed aside the documents to be proofread and fed a fresh paper into the typewriter. This would be the letter that would bring him home, once and for all. Alan couldn't live in Korea another year after seeing its real face.

Closing his eyes, Alan tried to will the darkness to come back and swallow up the guilt. How could the other men around him stomach what they did during their nights out? He was the furthest from divine love as he had ever been. The entire day passed as Alan sat in this agonized grasping for words, for the perfect articulation of apology, with nothing coming to mind.

Dear... the same starting line repeated down the page.

When Alan returned to the condo, Lester sat on the couch wearing a plain, short-sleeve shirt and track pants, settled in for a quiet night. A plastic basket sat on the coffee table.

"For you," Lester said, putting down the book he had been reading.

Alan came closer and saw that it contained a cake of soap, his razor, and towels.

"There's a bathhouse two neighborhoods over, a walkable distance. I'm prescribing you a nice, long soak, or else you really might summon the devil tonight," Lester said.

Beneath Lester's seemingly flyaway words, Alan understood enough the implication to wash away whatever was eating away at him. Lester shooed him out of the condo with one foot, absorbed back into his reading.

Knowing only that the bathhouse was two neighborhoods over, Alan wandered for a while, embarrassed by the plastic basket he held. Eventually, a wrinkled hand grabbed his shirttail and pulled Alan down the street in shuffling steps. They reached black brass gates, on which were mounted a wooden sign. The hand petted his shoulder and the man shuffled away.

Alan couldn't read the Korean writing, but the red squiggles representing steam provided indication enough that this was a bathhouse. Finding nothing to ring or indicate his presence, Alan pushed the gate open and entered.

A Korean girl sat on the steps, licking the frosting off a lopsided pink cake. Her short hair ended just below her ears, curling into her cheeks just so, and her eyes under their dark eyebrows were lowered to the cake.

"Excuse me, miss, is the bathhouse open?" Alan asked in English as he raised a palm to his slightly pulsing head. He could still barely put together a complete sentence in Korean even after all these years.

The girl looked up from the cake.

The screen with which he had seen everything for his whole life, blurred and indistinct, ran together into flinching and complete coherence, and this girl was at the center.

It hurt to look at her.

She was not a beautiful girl. The wide space between her eyes and her broad nose gave a vacant impression to her whole face, but her strong gaze was narrowed at him in laughter. She wore a green, bell-sleeve sweater, too vivid for the soft evening. Although Alan sensed she was laughing at him, he drew closer, wanting to make sense of the disharmony of her face, unpack her gaze.

"No kiss kiss," the girl bit out, misunderstanding his intentions. Alan smiled against the searing ache of the girl holding the cake. The phantom sweetness of frosting filled Alan's mouth. He swallowed and raised up his arms in surrender to her.

Alan mailed his last letter to the woman the next morning.

Dear, I'm sorry for the way I antagonized you those ten long years ago.

I found divine love, and ultimately it was not in you. For you see, the impossible has become possible, and my vision is clear. It was immediate and searing, it came in pain.

I can see!

People's faces are a wonder. Last night I came home and gripped my best friend's face in my hands to memorize his features. The most luminescent of faces, though, is that of my divine love. She will redeem and keep me. She will transcend my sin and the bounds of love as we know it, imperfect and mired in our parents' secrets.

It's all happening so fast. None of it makes sense, but I believe in this more than I have believed anything in my life. She and I, we will make our own life together in divine love. I'm going to treat her right this time. I will give her plenty of air. I'm going to marry her.

CHAPTER 7

Reunited with all her sisters and Daddy in the dining room, dinner was a perplexing affair for Yeo-deol after becoming accustomed to eating in isolation. She kept her head down as the platters moved down the table, embarrassed by her earlier outburst in the turret. The aroma of garlic and onion loosened her up enough to look up and see that Dul sat at the very end of the table after Yeol, the youngest. Set sat in Dul's usual seat next to Hana, and each girl had shifted up one seat.

"Hey, why is Du—" Yeo-deol's question cut off in a hiss of pain as Il-gop clamped a hand over Yeo-deol's delicate right arm.

"—Debussy so easy to slip over, Daddy? I think I should practice with Set on the piano," Il-gop said, propping up her chin. Her black eyes shined with amusement at Set's slight cough.

"Yes, that's a fantastic idea," Daddy said. He was cutting up the braised ribs on his plate into even smaller pieces, although the maids had already prepared them in bite sizes. The maids behind Daddy looked worried.

It became apparent to Yeo-deol what was happening as Il-gop stabbed up a triple portion of ribs with her fork and tipped half the platter of biscuits onto her plate. Il-gop made it the most obvious, but Hana, Set, Net, Da-seot, and Yeo-seot's plates were similarly heaped with more food than they could possibly eat. The most palpable emotion down the line of her sisters was surprisingly from Set, whose jaw was tensed over her full plate.

By the time the platters reached the end of the table, Dul spooned up the remaining scraps with glazed eyes. The aspect of Dul's shaved head cast her in a vulnerability that disgusted Yeo-deol. Who was this pathetic person? This wasn't her sister who had turned blue in the glass turret, refusing to open her mouth for air under Yeo-deol's hands.

The Dul that Yeo-deol knew must be lounging at the open window on the third floor at this very moment, Yeo-deol reasoned.

Daddy was making quite a sight from the head of the table. He ate wildly, gnashing the meat between his teeth and licking his fingers, the semblance of their father lost in hunger. Stunned, Yeo-deol felt her appetite drop away, seeing the churn of food mashed in Daddy's mouth. Only Yeo-seot could rival Daddy, which wasn't unusual, but her eyes were fixed on him with a hostility that Yeo-deol hadn't seen before, not her melancholy sister who stood in front of the record player to play Daddy his beloved songs.

Halfway through the dinner, Set whispered into Hana's ear briefly and stood up to leave the dining room. Maybe to go find the real Dul at the window upstairs, Yeo-deol thought with some satisfaction. Hana's face took on a contemplative expression between her brow as she glanced briefly at the end of the table.

Daddy didn't miss Set's exit. His posture was relaxed in his seat, but Yeo-deol saw how he followed Set's backside with his eyes. *Dugun…Dugun…Dugun.* The image of Daddy standing over Mama buried in the earth seized Yeo-deol's mind. She tasted dirt in her mouth.

She was right under our noses and we missed her, Yeo-deol, just like that, except it may be forever this time, Net's voice curled around Yeo-deol.

Yeo-deol shook her head fiercely and continued to chew her portion with difficulty in the festering silence.

Late that night when Daddy had surely gone to bed, Hana's voice in the dark of the turret ordered Da-seot and Yeo-seot to clear the floor of the blankets. Dul and Set hadn't come up after dinner for bed.

"Everything has changed again," Hana called as she exited the door. "Wait here."

Il-gop jostled Yeo-deol to sit on a pillow that she had dragged to the edge of the cleared circle. The other girls joined them in the same spot: Da-seot and Yeo-seot, and further apart, Net holding Yeol.

Yeo-deol had tried to talk to Net after dinner, sensing that she had upset her favorite sister by defending Dul. Net had been impenetrable, though, fussing over the strands of Yeo-seot's hair that had stuck together in the honey from dinner. Her doting attention on Yeo-seot blocked out all else, namely Yeo-deol, who squirmed next to her for a chance to apologize that never came.

The darkness of the turret let up as Yeo-deol's eyes adjusted. She waited with her sisters in anticipation as the muffled whispering continued outside the door. Hana re-entered the turret and stopped in the middle of the circle. She held a single candle in her hands, illuminating a small circle of her wide nose and lips poised with importance. Set stood by the door with her arms crossed over her chest, subject to Hana's ceremony as well.

"When we thought Yeo-deol would never wake up, we didn't know what to do. And it was *my* responsibility to decide as the eldest Henderson girl," Hana began, speaking in the air of a dictator addressing her nation rather than her pajama-clad sisters. "Were we supposed to throw Dul out the balcony? Demand that Daddy throw her out into the woods? As Il-gop said, though, it's wrong to kill a sister. But if we erase Dul as if she never existed, the problem disappears."

Yeo-deol balked. She remembered Net's earlier suggestion of getting rid of Dul like a dog. How a person could be erased, Yeo-deol couldn't grasp, and even if that was possible, it would be impossible to erase Dul. Dul, who in spite of the private violence she inflicted on Yeo-deol, effortlessly drew people's attention with her dark eyes and the intense, almost pure line of her movements.

All of Daddy's friends adored Dul. Whenever they visited to gather in Daddy's study, the girls lined up to greet them. "To show them how well-grown you are," Daddy would say. It wouldn't be pretty Da-seot they lingered around with her soft, open eyes and long lashes, or light-haired Il-gop, holding her violin in the loop of her arm. They stopped at Dul, stroking her dark hair and collarbone. The line of girls would only be broken through by Mama bearing a tray of scalding coffee and warm greetings.

"Everything has changed again," Hana repeated, "because Yeo-deol woke up, and not only that, she *forgave* Dul."

On cue with Hana's dramatics, Da-seot and Yeo-seot clapped enthusiastically. Yeo-deol shifted uncomfortably from where she sat, their applause pounding into her eardrums. In the glass of the teal door, she could see the waiting shadow of Dul.

At Hana's nod, Set opened the door. Dul entered, her head bowed, to join Hana in the middle of the circle. Her unsteady steps seemed to risk a floor that would crumble from under her feet without enough caution. Dul's hands were gathered around the stomach of her loose nightgown, like Mama did when her stomach swelled up with Yeol.

"Tonight, I have decided to let Dul back in with us, for Yeo-deol's sake. That means Dul is Dul again, Set is Set, Net is Net..." Hana proceeded through the list of girls, and at the last one, blew out the candle she held, sealing the ceremony in permanence. The girls waited in the darkness for what their reinstated sister would do. Dul lifted her hands away from her stomach, and a flat box hit the ground between Dul's feet. Leaning on their elbows and forearms, the girls watched as Hana picked up the package and worked off the wrapping. She pushed the box toward Yeo-deol for the official honor.

Yeo-deol lifted the lid, obscuring the contents from the awaiting girls, who pressed closer for a look. "What is it?" Yeo-seot asked urgently.

Pink blocks of candy dusted in white powder filled the vertical sleeve of the box.

"Turkish delight," Yeo-deol breathed, her sisters' eyes around her reflecting her own desire. They had only eaten it once before, after begging Mama for the candy that had enticed the boy to betray his siblings in the book she read to them. "You still want to eat the candy, knowing what the boy nearly gave in exchange? You're no better than the boy," Mama had said to the girls, worked up to a great frustration. She closed the book and read from the beginning of the story again. A few days later, though, each girl was served a square of the famed candy for dessert.

Wordlessly, all the girls reached in for a Turkish delight, and then a second, and then a third. It seemed the box was bottomless as their giggles and white powder wafted in the air. In the soft haze of sugar and impending drowsiness, Yeo-deol counted the sleeping lumps of her sisters. One was missing. *Ahop.*

As Yeo-deol drifted off, her breath froze to the blankets beneath her crawling with warmth. It was a multitude of Ahop-sized sleeping lumps making up her bed, and Yeo-deol was crushing Ahop from breathing fresh air. Sleep overtook Yeo-deol unwillingly.

Yeo-seot's hot breath fanned over Yeo-deol's face as she stirred awake. Under her long bangs, Yeo-seot blinked. "We need to talk," she said.

In the disorientation of sleep, Yeo-deol wondered if her sister wanted to eat her, run out of food at last. As Yeo-seot helped her sit up, Yeo-deol saw the other girls were still fast asleep, white powder ringing their mouths and wiped onto their clothes, evidence of Dul's redemption.

Yeo-deol let Yeo-seot lead her down the stairs, not used to such assertiveness from her melancholy sister. The trip was long, and Yeo-seot's breath gradually grew labored from the strain of supporting Yeo-deol on her crutches. It was an oddly touching sound for Yeo-deol, considering she and Yeo-seot weren't close. Admittedly, Yeo-seot wasn't close to any of the sisters, which seemed to simply come down to the fact that she alone sufficed at the record player.

"Are you hungry?" Yeo-deol spoke into the morning untouched yet by the other girls. Yeo-seot didn't answer.

Yeo-deol took the silence in stride, assuming she had asked an obvious question not worth answering, but Yeo-seot stopped to squeeze her hands around her narrow waist.

"I'm hungry so much, all the time, that it hurts," Yeo-seot whispered. "It's like my stomach has a hole, and I don't even taste the food. I'm just trying to fill up the hole."

It was true. The girls all saw that no matter how much Yeo-seot ate, her bones showed through her skin painfully. She was the skinniest of all the girls by no deliberate effort. During meals, the girls quietly passed over the remnants of their plates to Yeo-seot, who methodically ate through everything. Daddy said Yeo-seot had a fast metabolism and that it wasn't bad. However, the portions of the meals shrank so that the girls had less to give to Yeo-seot, probably by Daddy's order to the maids. Yeo-seot liked Mama's explanation better. She had called it *growing pains*: "It hurts to grow up, and Da-seot's pain is to eat, isn't it?"

They turned into the ballroom. Yeo-seot continued deeper into the immense darkness without turning on the lights by the double-set doors. Only the windows where the pale light of dawn showed through the fringes of the curtains vaguely marked the space.

"You know all this," Yeo-seot said to soothe Yeo-deol's uncertainty. She guided Yeo-deol's hand across smooth wood and the circular jut of several knobs. It was the record player; of course Yeo-seot had led them to the record player. It was too early to play anything, so they simply sat on the chilled floor.

"Daddy knew something was wrong between all of us, but he did nothing," Yeo-seot began, her voice thick with the disappointment of being let down by the person she adored the most in the world. Yeo-deol knew it didn't matter to Yeo-seot if she was Daddy's favorite. She strived to please Daddy in a love that sought nothing in return.

And then it hit Yeo-deol what had been so unnerving about Yeo-seot's hostility over last night's dinner. She had witnessed a transformation. Yeo-seot's flushed deference that Daddy and her sisters had taken for granted had been replaced by an objectivity that dared to directly look at and judge Daddy, who in his fragile ego had childishly interpreted it as a literal challenge to compete for food.

"It was like Hana said. She decided for all of us that Dul would be erased, so Set became Dul, Net became Set… Nobody knew their own names with the order all messed up. Daddy left us to become confused between ourselves," Yeo-seot continued.

"Did Hana do that to Dul's hair?" Yeo-deol asked. Her finger traced out the shape of Dul's scalp on the ground. Yeo-seot shook her head.

"Hana just likes to give orders, but it was Il-gop who suggested that we erase Dul first. When Daddy was occupied with the doctor, she trapped Dul under the dining table and reached in to shear Dul's hair off. Hana and Net closed off both ends of the table so that Dul couldn't escape."

"What about Set?"

Yeo-deol pictured Dul and Set smoking on opposite sides of their regular window, as if they had arrived at the same place by coincidence and decided to stay for the breeze.

"I went to go find her because surely she would come to Dul's defense. That's what you're thinking too, right?"

Yeo-seot shuddered a sigh that seemed to age her before Yeo-deol's very eyes.

"I found her at a window on the third floor, but not the regular one she and Dul usually stand at together. I pulled on her arm, telling her that Dul would die if she didn't do anything, but Set wouldn't budge. She just continued smoking out the window. Meanwhile, we could all hear Dul screaming for Mama."

Yeo-seot's stomach groaned between the two girls. A cry slipped from Yeo-deol's mouth, seeing Yeo-seot gnaw at her fist, the skin battered in bite marks. Not from hunger, but from the anxiety that churned in Yeo-seot's eyes.

"The worst part is that I'm no better. Because even after all that, Dul really did begin to get erased from my mind while you were in the pink room. I had so much difficulty remembering why we were visiting you, or how you got injured in the first place. It's so much easier to erase a person in your mind than you think. You just need to have the determination. I was determined not to look at the end of the table, where she sat. And who knows who'll be in that seat next? Maybe it'll be you or me."

CHAPTER 8

———

On the stairs looking into the darkened foyer, Yeo-deol peeked into the pin-striped hat box on her lap, checking that the remaining squares of Turkish delight and Dr. Roberts's newest gift for her, chocolates coiled into shapes of circus animals, were in place. "I'll take you one day," he had promised this morning, arranging the animals in a fantastical array of the circus show atop his black notebook. The doctor had ruffled Yeo-deol's hair when she asked if all her sisters could go as well. "The house would fall apart if all you girls left at once," he said. She glared into the weak lie.

Yeo-deol had formulated a plan. It wasn't a great plan, resorting to waiting for Net to come downstairs for dinner and holding her hostage by her ankles. Yeo-deol hoped the hat box would soften up Net, who had been evading Yeo-deol entirely over the past few days. Yeo-deol woke up alone in the mornings. She missed the *clack clack clack* of the stolen peppermint candies in Net's secret hem that used to dredge Yeo-deol up from sleep.

Net was nowhere to be found in their usual haunts, not in the circular bed on the third floor or the maids' quarters. She had even checked Mama's room, but only breathed in dust. Yeo-deol had searched today, too, tapping on her crutches through the house that seemed to expand with more rooms each day. Net's evasion was a game of cunning, always just out of Yeo-deol's reach. Yeo-deol heard her older sister everywhere: in the soft tread of footprints a floor above, three doors down, and the slightest sound of a shutting door.

Without any desire to pick up her pastels or paints, Yeo-deol spent the hours of daylight shivering on the balcony and catching snow in her hair until the sky darkened enough to begin the long descent down the stairs. In the dining room, Yeo-deol sat as the maids laid out the silverware and plates. Her sisters and Daddy gradually took their places at the table, and Net appeared last of all, her arms full with a glowering Yeol and a Yeo-seot wilting with hunger.

The break between Yeo-deol and Net inevitably rippled into the other girls' routines. The maids whispered about how Ahop had apparently woken up briefly to ask a shocked maid where Mama was before going back to sleep. Il-gop told Daddy she sickened of playing the violin, which Daddy could not accept. "If you lack self-discipline, you'll lose your music," Daddy had said as he closed Il-gop this time into the pink room.

The records Yeo-seot played went from mournful winter sonatas to blazing concertos that rang through the house. "Turn that damn thing down!" Daddy's voice would yell distantly, and Yeo-seot's obedience surpassed his command. The agonized sound of the record player skimming on air stretched through the entire house until Yeo-seot dropped the needle back down.

Da-seot clung tighter to Hana, encircling her arms around Hana's waist and planting her feet atop Hana, who uncharacteristically tolerated it, stepping into a one-person waltz to the music. Even Dul and Set stood closer to one another at their usual window in recent days, handing a shared cigarette back and forth.

"Seo-ah?" Daddy's voice broke over Yeo-deol from the base of the stairs.

Yeo-deol squinted into the dim light at the foreign name. Her name, Soo-ah, her real name that she only faintly remembered Mama calling her, was similar but not exactly the same.

"No, Daddy, I'm Yeo-deol," she tried to say, but her words thinned to a whistling that could have come from the night outside. The moon was visible through the windowpane above the door in the foyer.

Daddy came up the stairs to her cautiously, the way Net crept up to small animals in the summer. He knelt down in front of Yeo-deol and touched the crutches she had secured through the railings. It almost felt like he was afraid to look at her face.

"How long have you been here?" Daddy asked, clasping their hands together.

Yeo-deol vaguely remembered Dr. Roberts telling her to not travel up and down the stairs alone, that she could become stuck so easily or worse. Daddy must have assumed she was stuck on the stairs. A part of her feared he might put her away in the pink room again, where Il-gop already unhappily spent the days practicing her violin.

"Not very long," Yeo-deol answered, tentatively taking in Daddy's response.

Daddy's hands tightened over hers.

"Where have you been? What have you been doing?"

"I've been waiting here," Yeo-deol said, looking behind her at the darkness from where Net would hopefully emerge. She startled as Daddy bowed his head onto her lap, pushing out the hatbox onto the step below. A powdered heap of Turkish delight and cracked chocolates spilled out from the tipped box at her feet.

"Have we gone so far that we've come back to the beginning?" Daddy's voice was muffled into her skirt, which was slowly dampening with tears. He was still mistaking Yeo-deol for someone else.

No, Daddy, I'm Yeo-deol. Yeo-deol swallowed, trying to reach the simple clarification that eluded her, like grasping at a thought before the words took form. The weight of Daddy's head felt disproportionately heavy to what her shaking legs could hold up. Just as her legs were about to give out, the doorbell rang.

Daddy lifted his head and stared at the front door. The doorbell rang again.

As he swiftly went down the stairs to answer the door, Yeo-deol could hear her approaching sisters, emerging from the rooms above and in the long hallway below leading into the foyer. Knees brushed Yeo-deol's back as some of her sisters settled behind her. Hana, Da-seot, and Yeo-seot leaned against the wall along the base of the stairs, presumably having come from the ballroom.

Yeo-deol stiffened as Net sat next to her with an indifferent gaze locked forward, as if to deny Yeo-deol's presence despite choosing to sit in the spot. Yeol was nestled in Net's arms, her tiny hands clenched in a threat at the outward world.

Daddy opened the door.

Yeo-deol and her sisters gasped at the first thing they saw: a magnificent tower of yellow boxes, each tied with a pink satin ribbon. Yeo-deol counted down the vertical pile, anxious at its precarious sway. There were ten boxes, one for each girl.

"I have presents, presents for all of my girls!"

Auntie's face appeared from behind the boxes.

Not one of the girls stirred, their eyes turned to Daddy for permission. Auntie's eyes nervously switched to Daddy, too, who stayed fixed in his spot. Yeo-deol's fingers agitated to touch the smooth ribbon and rip away the beautiful paper. She had never seen such a shade of yellow before, so soft and luminescent, like a memory of the sun superior to the real one.

"Out," Daddy said. The girls followed his outstretched hand, only to realize he was pointing at them. Hana's eyes hardened at this unexpected switch, but she obeyed with her hands that herded Da-seot and Yeo-seot back into the ballroom. Il-gop edged past Yeo-deol from where she had been sitting behind her to join them.

Daddy had already turned back to Auntie.

Yeo-deol looked up as Net rose, silently pleading for help getting to her feet. Net smiled softly for a moment, a tenderness that Yeo-deol hadn't seen even in their former closeness, and then she proceeded down the stairs, leaving Yeo-deol alone.

Daddy and Auntie's faces were so close together that they were obscured perfectly by the pile of yellow boxes. Yeo-deol looked behind her to see not all of her sisters had left as she had thought. Set sat farther up the stairs, watching the scene at the doorway in deep concentration. Set didn't acknowledge Yeo-deol except with the slightest lift of her chin. *Watch*, she was saying to Yeo-deol, *there's something worth watching here.*

"Why did you come back?" Daddy said, deflecting his odd tone of questioning onto Auntie as Yeo-deol crawled up the stairs to where Set was.

"I ran and ran, but no matter how far I seemed to go, I came back here," Auntie said.

The nape of Yeo-deol's neck tensed in terror as her grip on the step above her slipped. Set rescued her, pulling up Yeo-deol by her uninjured wrist onto the step she had been sitting on. At Set's chosen height, Yeo-deol could see Daddy and Auntie's faces angled around the boxes.

The shape of Daddy's mouth spoke words too low for Yeo-deol to discern, but it was as if every hue of Auntie darkened in distress, from her hazel eyes to her flushed cheeks that accepted each and every word to her core. Yeo-deol wanted to rescue Auntie from her own daddy. Next to her, Set's eyes were narrowed in a stare that seemed to want to pin down the whole of Auntie onto the floor of the foyer, a needle to each limb.

The yellow boxes toppled down in a wincing crash.

Daddy grabbed Auntie in a hug, his head slumped onto her shoulder. Daddy looked so tired, so exhausted, with the front door open behind them. Yeo-deol blinked at what she first thought was small tufts of snow falling, but the night sky was bare of the looming fullness of snow clouds. Dust, Yeo-deol realized, dispersed around them in the air.

When Yeo-deol looked down, the yellow boxes were scattered around the emptied doorway, and the last of Auntie's outstretched hand disappeared into the darkness of the hallway.

Dugun.

Set knelt down on the step below Yeo-deol, offering her back. She didn't seem to notice the falling dust around them, as slight as it was. Yeo-deol awkwardly wrapped her arms around Set's neck. They hadn't talked since the night Set led her to Mama's emptied pantry. Instead of joining the other girls' silence in the ballroom, Set went up the stairs.

"Where was Auntie going?" Yeo-deol whispered.

"Wherever Daddy wanted to take her," Set answered, without elaborating further.

"What do you think about her?"

Yeo-deol remembered the way Auntie smiled with her whole face the first morning.

"She disgusts me," Set said.

Yeo-deol had nothing to say to that, the image of the outstretched hand creeping back to her mind. Whether the hand was reaching out from the darkness, or stretching out to escape it, Yeo-deol wasn't sure.

Set lowered Yeo-deol onto the floor. They had arrived at Dul and Set's window on the third floor. Dul had been waiting for them, turning a box of cigarettes in her hands. A floral scarf hung loosely off Dul's shoulders. Da-seot had tied it over Dul's shaved head in the morning, and Dul had let her, though once Da-seot ran off to wherever Hana was, she slipped it off.

Dul's shaved head appeared fuller already, which Yeo-deol took comfort in. She wasn't as scared of Dul as she used to be since trying to choke her in the turret. It was like Yeo-deol and Dul acknowledged that the score had become evened between them now.

Dul handed Set a cigarette. As Set stepped up to open the windows, Yeo-deol was surprised when Dul offered her one too. Yeo-deol shook her head and Dul shrugged, turning for the light. Yeo-deol sat there as her sisters smoked, appreciating the nothingness that transpired between them that for some reason she was allowed to take part in.

The girls kept their heads down throughout dinner. They restrained their prior hostility toward Auntie, understanding the meaning of Daddy's choice in the foyer. Auntie was above them now, yet more so, there was a hesitation because she hadn't simply come back. The maids had decked out Auntie in Mama's extravagance. Her hair was longer, the wet tendrils running down her back in a seemingly impossible length for the weeks she had been gone. In place of the green sweater or any of the maids' clothes, Auntie wore a translucent silk slip the color of milk, embroidered with purple flowers. Every turn of her head seemed to glisten with drops of diamonds that floated in her black hair.

Seeing Auntie like this, it was hard to believe that their Mama hadn't come back to them. *Same but different enough to feel wrong.* Net's regret weighed on Yeo-deol, who increasingly struggled to recall Mama's exact features, except for her dark eyes that matched her dark hair. How could Yeo-deol struggle to recognize Mama behind her beautiful dresses and the jangle of her jewelry? It shouldn't have been this difficult.

Yeo-deol watched her sisters pick at the Black Forest cake, their favorite dessert, which they had been anticipating for the entire day. The pantry key in Yeo-deol's possession had lost its power once she flatly declared, "I ate all of it, down to the last crumb. The pantry's entirely empty," bringing Da-seot and Yeo-seot to tears. Hana had paled and backed out of the room, silently caught and called out in her con. Yet, Hana's deception had tainted the taste of all desserts for the girls by the sole fact that it wasn't Mama's baking.

Auntie ate her slice oblivious to the tension, popping a cherry off its stem. Her light eyes softened into the sweetness of the whipped cream, as if it was her first time eating cake. Yeo-deol scooped up a forkful of the cream and let it sit on her tongue, trying to taste what Auntie was tasting. Daddy stared at Auntie too as his throat bobbed down red wine. *No, Daddy, that's not Mama,* Yeo-deol thought.

CHAPTER 9

———

The glass turret cramped with the bumping of bony shoulders and the quiet drag of individual blankets in a silent fight for floor space. The sense of being cramped that night was heightened by the return of Hana, Da-seot, and Il-gop, who had slept in the ballroom apart from the other girls every night since Mama went away, aside for the special ceremony reinstating Dul as their sister.

Yeo-deol wondered if they were spooked by Auntie's presence in the house, even if Hana or Il-gop's pride would never let them admit so.

Of course, Hana stopped in the middle of the room to give an elaborate explanation.

"We couldn't sleep in the ballroom, not at night. It's so cold in there that our skin began to turn blue," Hana said, her distant eyes probably reveling in the romanticism of withering away in the ballroom like a flower.

She rotated out her arms to demonstrate their blue pallor, but Yeo-deol saw the same sallow tone the girls collectively took on during winter without much sun. The other girls, Dul, Set, Net, and Yeo-seot, likewise frowned, not seeing anything out of the ordinary.

"Can't you see it?" Hana asked, picking up on her sisters' skepticism.

Da-seot and Il-gop stood to the side and stared at their bare feet, neither speaking up or denying their experience sleeping in the ballroom.

"I'm telling the truth," Hana insisted, looking down at her arms at what apparently she alone could see. It was strange, the lengths she was going to maintain this deception, Yeo-deol thought. Yet all she could hear from Hana's mouth were lies after seeing Mama's emptied pantry for herself and learning about the petty scheme manipulating the girls' subservience.

Lacking anything to say, the girls resumed the bustle of preparing for bed, enveloping Hana out of sight from where Yeo-deol sat with her back to the cool glass wall, loosening and tightening a roll of blank paper to distract herself. Her stomach churned with the Black Forest cake from dinner.

The whipped cream that Yeo-deol had melted onto her tongue earlier felt like it had hardened into a slick ball in her gut. If she didn't spit it out now, Yeo-deol feared it would stay inside her and expand like a balloon, slowing down her movements day by day until one day she just stopped.

None of her sisters noticed as a potent wave of drowsiness bowed Yeo-deol into the blankets below her. Her last thought was of Mama's emptied cabinet again. *Everything is poisoned in this house.*

Yeo-deol sighed into the unfurling of her consciousness.

Dugun... Dugun... Dugun...

A luminescence flared through Yeo-deol's eyelids. She opened her eyes to the flat aspect of a red sun. Sitting up in cold sand, Yeo-deol wondered if someone had dimmed the sun from moments ago. Shivering, she looked out to a shallow ocean that stretched out to a teal horizon matching the turret door. The wavy air emulated a summer day without actual heat, and she was further confused by her toes, which were dipped into warm water. Yeo-deol was evidently no longer in the glass turret.

The more Yeo-deol let the details settle around her, the more she recognized this mixed-up place. The sandy bank, the oversaturated colors of the water and sun, and the feeling of the water. This was the island that Yeo-deol had plummeted into from the balcony, where her bones had hewn in the water and she had found Daddy in a deep slumber.

To Yeo-deol's relief, Daddy was gone now, and as she climbed further up the sloping bank of sand, she saw that the gnarled orange tree was gone also. There was but a jagged hole left in the ground, and the entrails of red roots coiling out of the former spot suggested that the orange tree had been violently uprooted without any trail of debris in the water or sky.

A swelling in the ground caused Yeo-deol to stumble. It was a mound of sand in the ground. There were several of them encircling the former spot of the orange tree. Squatting down to the first mound, Yeo-deol spoke, more to hear her own voice in this hushed place.

"It's so lonely here. I'd like to go home now, please," she said to the mound.

Sometimes in dreams like this that went on for too long, all it took to reorient herself was to speak out loud what she wanted to happen next.

"I want to go home. Home, home, home," Yeo-deol repeated, lowering her head over the mound. She closed her eyes, determined to go back to sleep and wake up in the turret again.

The mound tremored a low-pitched hum in her ears, a sweet sound that Yeo-deol felt she had heard a long time ago. The hum died away when Yeo-deol raised her head to hear only the gentle lapping of water on the shore. Yeo-deol pressed her ear back to the mound, and the hum resumed in her chest this time, warming and loosening the knot in her stomach. Laughing along the different mounds, Yeo-deol found each one hummed at a slightly different pitch.

The mounds in the circle progressively shrank in size. One mound with a hollowed middle was silent. Yeo-deol thought another squat mound was silent, but when she leaned in closer, she heard a faint whistling of air. Eleven mounds, she counted, like the tinfoil stars that hung in the pink room.

Circled back to the first mound, Yeo-deol occupied herself with making a bed in the sand. Her ears echoed with the hums that blended into Mama's smoky timbre in which she sang lullabies.

A scream erupted from the mound, knocking Yeo-deol off her feet.

The screaming seemed to rise from the ground and shake the whole circumference of the island. It didn't relent, lashing into Yeo-deol's eardrums as she splashed into the water and ran without looking back.

The clap of silence came as abruptly as the screaming began. Yeo-deol's legs gave out under her, and she landed in the water that had remained level to her ankle. When she turned around, the island was no longer visible. She had outrun the island and the screaming mound.

Yeo-deol trudged forward in the direction she faced, weighed down by the soaked material of her nightgown. She was the sole break in the expanse of the teal ocean. There were no dinner bells or sisters to give meaning to the passing time. The frill of Yeo-deol's neckline dried stiff as she walked through what must have been the remainder of winter and maybe even the beginning of spring. Spring, when Daddy said Mama could come home.

The *could* bothered Yeo-deol, as if Daddy was putting the choice on Mama.

A yellow spot appeared in the horizon. Yeo-deol broke into an eager jog, waving her arms frantically as she drew closer to the spot that formed into a yellow house on wooden stilts. A couple sat in the front of the house with their legs hanging off the dock.

"Mama?" Yeo-deol said in disbelief at the unmistakable visage. She ran to close the remaining distance, her feet a frantic blur in the water, until she stopped below Mama and the man in her arms. The man was not Daddy.

Is this where you've been all along, Mama?

Yeo-deol rubbed away her tears angrily. Mama hadn't been buried in the ground or transposed into Auntie. She had emptied the pantry and left in the night without taking anything to come here. She had left them all heartbroken, the other girls and Daddy.

The heat of Yeo-deol's anger passed, and she calmed down enough to think more rationally. First of all, she didn't know exactly where this place was, and Daddy had told the girls that Mama left for a trip. Had Yeo-deol somehow stumbled into Mama's faraway trip? Of all the possibilities she had pondered so far, this was the most comforting.

"Mama!" Yeo-deol yelled through her cupped hands. Mama didn't seem to be able to hear her at the height of the stilt house. Yeo-deol walked around the perimeter of the stilt house, searching for a means to climb up. When she returned to the point she began, there was a flight of wooden stairs that hadn't been there before. Yeo-deol frowned at the strangeness but quickly set aside her doubts to hurry up the stairs. At the top, Yeo-deol couldn't contain her gasp at the view. It was like the whole world was a simple sheet of blue water, and she was in the middle of it. Mama and the man sat facing away from Yeo-deol as she approached them.

"*Dong-ju, wake up, I'm bored,*" Mama said in Korean.

Yeo-deol tipped her head, unwilling to believe her ears. Yeo-deol didn't know Korean, and neither did any of her sisters.

"*What should we eat for dinner tonight?*" another sentence floated in the air.

Korean was Mama's private language from which she infrequently plucked out a word or phrase to teach them. *Precious. The mugunghwa flowers have bloomed. House. Family. I'm sorry. Fate. I love you.* Yeo-deol and the other girls had Korean names of their own that had long slipped their minds, and Mama made no point of reminding them.

Yeo-deol sank down next to Mama, whose arms cradled a strange man. By his black hair and the curve of his closed eyes, he could have been Mama's secret brother with how similar he looked to Mama, more than any of the girls put together. That could have explained why Mama was holding a man other than Daddy. Yet the entanglement of their limbs and breath was that of lovers.

Mama didn't acknowledge Yeo-deol's presence, absorbed in a whispered conversation with the sleeping man that pointedly excluded Yeo-deol.

"Hi, Mama," Yeo-deol began, the churn of everything she had to say more urgent than the sting of Mama's uncharacteristic snub. When she looked at Mama properly, the gush of words dried up. This wasn't her Mama.

Not Mama who powdered herself to a ghostly pallor and wore tissue paper-like gowns. Not Mama who sat nightly at her dresser, rubbing lotions and oils into her skin. Not Mama, who smiled widely for Daddy's friends with platters of poisoned cakes.

This Mama was browned from the sun, and dressed in jean cut-offs and a shapeless shirt that bulged at her stomach. The black eyes staring out to the ocean were unchanged, eyes that Yeo-deol hoped she would grow into, intent to scrutinize and strip things to their core. The girls had never been among those "things," but Yeo-deol had seen the way Daddy's friends shifted uncomfortably and laughed too loudly under her gaze.

The eyes, nose, cheekbones, and face shape that Yeo-deol had immediately picked out from a distance were all arranged correctly, but close-up it was like the lines of her body and features had been threaded by a string and pulled tight in a clenched fist. This was Mama in her youth before the fist had started to slacken, and Yeo-deol connected, whom

Auntie resembled uncannily. Same but different enough to feel wrong.

This rougher Mama with the same black eyes was radiant. The lines on her face melted into a happiness coloring across her sun-browned cheekbones. Yeo-deol bowed her head, wondering if she had ever seen Mama smile like this.

"Mama..." Yeo-deol trailed off, uncertain now even in this address.

Tired of being ignored, she resorted to shaking Mama's arm for attention, the very kind of action that would usually result in a scolding from Daddy. Mama repositioned herself, turning away her body, as if Yeo-deol was an insistent breeze, and it occurred to her that Mama honestly may not be able to see her right there.

The jostling stirred the man, whose head lolled to Yeo-deol's side. His slow blinks opened up to a gentle impressionability that Yeo-deol wanted to cover up with her palms, so as to not allow it to become spoiled. Leaning in for a closer look, Yeo-deol touched her nose to his and turned her head back and forth.

"This is how people in some parts of the world greet one another," Yeo-deol whispered, echoing one of Daddy's friends, whom she had watched greet Dul in such a way from a shadowed corner.

"What's so interesting on that side?" Mama asked.

"The air is sweeter here," the man said as he drew back to Mama.

"Sweeter than me?"

Mama was teasing, but there was an edge of expectation in his answer.

"*Definitely. You're a bitter orange that I always spit out at first, because I'm not supposed to eat it out of hand.*"

The man grinned at Mama's light slap on his chest. She didn't move away her hand.

"*But I love its raw acidity and how it wakes me up. I'll always choose the bitter orange until I grow sick, and then I'll wait for the sickness to pass and eat it again,*" he said.

The man scooted out of Mama's hold and stretched out his arms in a yawn.

Yeo-deol gripped the wooden railing above her as Mama's arms were pulled into the arc of his motion. Both their hands were conjoined to each other, as if facing a mirrored reflection. They stood up and worked together to pull each other's shirts off.

The bulge of Mama's exposed stomach strained against her skin. Yeo-deol hated how vulnerable and soft it was, how easy it would be for someone to lay their hands there and squash it.

Yeo-deol hastily sat on her hands and averted her attention to the water below. One by one, discarded articles of clothing dropped in. Amidst the floating objects, there was an odd object that resembled a mask, a familiar face that had its eyes and mouth hollowed out. Yeo-deol firmly shook her head to chase out the grotesque suggestion.

A piece of fabric fluttered to the edge of the dock. Yeo-deol picked it up and flushed, seeing that it was Mama's underwear, warmed from the sun like the rest of her. Not wanting anyone else to find it, Yeo-deol stuffed it in her dress pocket. Her eyes were growing heavy with the hit of drowsiness beyond her control again.

"*Dong-ju*," Mama's sigh carried in the breeze.

Yeo-deol staggered past the entangled couple toward the yellow house. Skimming her hand on the tin roof that came up to her waist, Yeo-deol climbed through the window and somersaulted into a pitch-black darkness.

Dugun... Dugun... Dugun...

CHAPTER 10

—

The darkness lifted off Yeo-deol, hardening and taking shape into the familiar layout of the foyer, yet the details here had shifted too. The walls were papered with a vivid print of green leaves that Yeo-deol squinted at, not sure if the bristling in her ears was real. Wilting flowers coloring white, purple, and red spotted the vegetation.

It was like the house had been left to bloom in the wild for several centuries.

Dugun ... Dugun ... Dugun ...

The cracks in the marble floor under Yeo-deol's hands ran up to the yellow boxes that were scattered in front of the door. There were nine, meaning one had been claimed or stolen. The yellow wrapping that had looked so sleek just the previous night was soiled by smudges of orange and brown, as if something was rotting inside, and indeed, it smelled like it. The longer Yeo-deol sat in the stench, though, the sweeter it turned in her nose.

Sweet, like Black Forest cake.

Sweet, like orange slices before the nauseating turn.

A squeamish sound came from above Yeo-deol, who tilted her chin up. A hand gripped the stairway railing, the knuckles bared white. Unable to see who it was and uncertain if she wanted to know, the walk to the base of the stairs was agonizing for Yeo-deol. The black glut of cream dripped into each leaden lift of her feet until she was planted at the bottom step.

As if this was a game with one of her sisters, Yeo-deol counted up the steps:

One step, two step, three step, four.

Five step, six step, seven step, eight.

On the ninth step, Daddy caged in Auntie against the railing. The tip of his tongue slid out and licked up a spot of whip cream on Auntie's lips.

"You will do," Daddy's voiceless whisper rose in a mist to Yeo-deol's ears.

Under the bend of Daddy's arm, Auntie's rounded eyes fixed on Yeo-deol. She relinquished no emotion on her face aside from the grit of her teeth, yet it was like Auntie's tears seeped through Yeo-deol's body, loosening the glut in her stomach.

A gush of black poured out of Yeo-deol's mouth. She clapped her hands over her mouth, but she couldn't stop the stream of the sticky black substance that continued to flow through the gaps of her fingers onto the floor, rising to her ankles, then her waist, and then her chin. As the foyer was wiped away in a black ocean, hands closed over Yeo-deol.

Dugun ... Dugun ... Dugun ...

"Shhh, it's just me, you idiot."

It was Dul's voice.

Yeo-deol's body felt split between two polarities of temperatures, dampened in sweat from the nightmarish dream spilling into the darkness around her while shaking in an unbearable chill.

"Where, where are we?" Yeo-deol struggled to enunciate through her chattering teeth.

She wondered if this was a new form of torture by Dul. It was cold enough that Dul might have dragged Yeo-deol outside into the snow, or to a less extreme possibility, perhaps sufficed herself with the room-sized freezer in which the maids stored the meats and tubs of ice cream.

It seemed like Dul had mellowed out after being brought back from nothing. Smug in the shared moment at Dul and Set's window, Yeo-deol had gone beyond to entertain that she had earned Dul's respect after almost killing her in the turret.

"See for yourself," Dul said callously, implacable in the dark, but she was close.

As Yeo-deol's eyes adjusted to the gloom, she saw the lusterless crystals of a chandelier overhead, and the familiar horn of Yeo-seot's record player. They were inside the ballroom.

"Why did you bring me here?" Yeo-deol asked.

"You were the one writhing in the foyer. I thought you were having a seizure or something, but it stopped, thankfully. I would've carried you back up to the turret. I'm just so tired," Dul said, her voice thinning out.

Yeo-deol could barely make out Dul's form slumped against the wall in the darkness. Dul's teeth faintly chattered in the cold as well, a much more human sister than the one who used to embody terror for Yeo-deol. There was a greater force at work tormenting them, beyond the tortures they inflicted onto one another.

Sick of the darkness, sick of the whiplash of place and familiarity, Yeo-deol rose to her feet and limped to where the windows began. She picked up the cord threading through the heavyset curtains and pulled—the effort usually requiring several maids together. The veins in Yeo-deol's neck strained as the curtains swept open an increment. That had been all she wanted.

The moon shone through the gap in the curtain, illuminating the dust balls floating across the floor in a strip of light. Yeo-deol clumsily ambled back to Dul, comforted by the growing ache of her right ankle that was evidence of her being awake. Leaning on each other, she and Dul walked to the sliver of light that Yeo-deol had made for them.

"I took the elevator to find you," Dul heaved. "It's like this place is never-ending. I stopped on every imaginable floor, every possible room, more than our house should be able to fit. I spent so much time lost that I was sure that witch got to you."

Yeo-deol couldn't forget Auntie's terror underneath Daddy, the tears she had poured into Yeo-deol's body. The chase was becoming entangled, and it was unclear who was chasing whom.

"I don't think it's as simple as that," Yeo-deol said.

They had reached the open curtain. Dul lay down on the ground onto the strip of light. Yeo-deol blinked and blinked one more time to make sure she was seeing right.

"Dul, are you having trouble breathing?"

"What are you talking about?" Dul said. Her eyes flickered up to Yeo-deol, appearing perfectly fine despite the fact that her face had taken on the same blue pallor from suffocating under Yeo-deol's hands in the turret.

Numbly, Yeo-deol raised her own hands and saw that her flesh was cast in blue. It was no trick of light, not where they sat in the light. Hana had been telling the truth about the coldness and the blue skin in the ballroom.

"Shit," Dul said, seeing Yeo-deol's hand, but her drowsy eyes were closing.

Yeo-deol cuddled up next to Dul, closing her fingers around her sister's slackened hand.

Thank you for coming to save me, Yeo-deol thought as she warily let sleep overtake her again. In her pocket, she felt Mama's sun-warmed underwear.

This time, she dreamt of nothing. Nothing was a spread of white in which she suspended the fragments of herself, without body or name or place. The final peace of nothing-ness clawed up her throat. *I'm not ready for this yet.*

Yeo-deol bolted awake to darkness. The moon had shifted, taking away the column of light from the window. Wrapping her arms tighter around Dul, Yeo-deol laid awake and waited for the night to pass.

In the early morning before even the maids were up to prepare breakfast, Yeo-deol and Dul slipped into the din-ing room and left each other alone in their separate seats. Yeo-deol stared at the trace of blue that had faded down to her fingertips.

Net entered the dining room first, missing her usual armload of Yeol. The hand wrapped around her wrist and the red teeth marks up her forearm told of a defeat this morn-ing to tame their temperamental sister. Net's eyes narrowed momentarily, drifting between Dul and Yeo-deol, before her expression cooled into a mask of geniality. The faint *clack clack clack* of Net's skirt as she took her seat pained Yeo-deol, who freshly remembered her reconciliatory offering crushed under Daddy's feet.

"Good morn—" Yeo-deol began to say.

"Yeol counted up to *four* in Korean yesterday," Net cut off Yeo-deol, turning to Dul. The comment was obviously directed at Yeo-deol, rubbing her replacement into her face.

Yeo-deol sighed. She was growing exhausted of this mind game.

Considering Yeol as her replacement didn't inspire jealousy in Yeo-deol, but rather gave her the distance to bluntly scrutinize the doting that she had accepted so naturally. Net possessed the devotion and exclusivity of a mother's love that had been comforting at her side. Except Net's love twisted into the need to monopolize, and Yeo-deol had unintentionally gone against her.

"Going to teach her your thieving ways next?" Dul asked, tapping the top of the jam knife into the table cloth. Net's hand poised over her fork dangerously.

The idle chatter and movement of chairs of the other girls filing into the dining room drowned out the mounting tension. Yeo-deol watched for Hana's familiar head among the girls, resolved to apologize to her after breakfast. Hana's seat remained empty, though.

"I thought she was with Dul and Yeo-seot," Da-seot said once all the girls were seated.

Yeo-deol looked down the table at Dul, who looked just as confused as her.

"Maybe she's preparing a surprise performance and forgot about the time."

"She got in trouble with Daddy because he wanted the pantry key back."

"What if Daddy finally gave her a sleeping room of her own?"

As the girls became enraptured in their theories, Daddy and Auntie entered the room. Daddy glowed with a summer jubilance, outfitted in a tan suit and pale blue tie like he was going to step onto a boat. It was a discomfiting contrast to Auntie's drawn face, even more so that her pale blue dress matched Daddy's tie color.

Nine pairs of eyes watched Daddy lead Auntie by the small of her back into Mama's seat opposite his place at the table. Set gripped a water cup in her hands, pressuring the glass with a strength indiscernible but by the tremor of her braid. Of all the girls, Set probably hated Auntie the most because she had loved Mama the best.

"I wonder what has shut up the buzz around my little flowers?" Daddy asked as he walked back to his chair. Although his tone was casual, lighthearted even, the challenge was clear. He was giving them the opportunity to speak up.

The other girls looked at one another, lacking the words to describe the wrongness they were witnessing. They busied themselves with eating. Yeo-deol found the words, but stuffed them back down with a croissant and handfuls of raspberries. To voice the wrongness would be to give it a reality, the wrongness that Daddy was replacing Mama with Auntie in a repulsive mirroring of Net's replacement of Yeo-deol.

"Daddy, where did Hana go?" Da-seot asked through her full mouth.

"Ah, wipe the worry from your eyes—and there, in the corner of your mouth, love. Hana fell sick in the night from eating too many of Mama's pastries," Daddy said.

This time, the nine pairs of eyes fixed on Daddy at the brazen lie to which he was oblivious.

"All of a sudden?" Set's voice sliced through the air softly.

Daddy's eyes widened at the rare address by his silent daughter.

"Yes, it was very sudden," he stammered and cleared his throat.

"Well, let's all go and visit Hana after breakfast, make sure she's recovering nicely," Dul said, tipping back on her chair legs.

"No, no, Hana's in a *secret* place because we need to keep her sickness contained. After all, I can't have all my girls withering on me, can I?" Daddy said.

A cracking sound dug into Yeo-deol's ears.

She covered her hands over her ears, but the rest of her sisters, Daddy, and Auntie carried on with their breakfast unaffected. Dul frowned at Yeo-deol, seeing her distress. At Dul's elbow, she had confiscated the glass cup intact from Set's hands.

Yeo-deol began to feel woozy.

The focus of her vision inverted, blurring out the foreground of her sisters and closing in the large windows in the background. Across the windows, the fractures that had been eating into her ears were materializing, deep gashes through which the wind whistled, incomparable to the hairline fractures before in the turret.

Yeo-deol kept her eyes fastened on the windows, not knowing what went into her mouth. She breathlessly waited for the glass to shatter down on them. Would everyone else in the room still bleed from a rain of shards they couldn't see? The moment didn't come, however. Instead, a fog spread across the cracked glass and solidified into a protective sheet. It would be okay for now.

Yeo-deol blinked. Drawn back to the dining room, she looked around and saw that the chairs at the table had emptied out except for Auntie and her.

"They're in the foyer," Auntie said, referring to her sisters, "The maids mentioned something about new dresses from Mama, and that's all it took for them to run."

Mama? Had she returned from her trip? Was everything going to return to normal?

There was a change in Auntie, being alone with her like this. Her muted demeanor with Daddy had loosened into the openness that sat so prettily on her face, livening up her cheeks and hazel eyes. There were croissant flakes stuck around her mouth.

"You didn't leave with Daddy?"

Auntie's eyes seemed to dim a little at the mention of him, and she shrugged stiffly.

"I don't need to follow your father around everywhere. I wanted to sit a bit longer, so I did," she said with an edge in her voice.

"You looked so scared sitting here, like you were waiting for something bad to happen," Auntie continued in a more gentle tone that could have been concern.

"I think something is poisoning our house. I can taste it in my food, I see it in my dreams, I can hear it slowly breaking through windows all around me," Yeo-deol said.

Auntie's mouth twitched at the thinly veiled implication.

Her gaze had gone cold, shuttered closed again, as her hands worked the corner of the tablecloth into knots. Those unknowable eyes looked up to the windows, sweeping along the cracks that she had been able to see all along.

A murky image rippled to the surface of Yeo-deol's mind of Auntie hunting for something. She had created the picture while lonesome in the pink room, paying no mind to the meaning that now sank into Yeo-deol's chest.

She needed to leave the dining room, away from this woman who tugged on her sympathy with the crumbs around her mouth, yet menaced her by what she withheld. Last night in the ballroom, Yeo-deol had told Dul that Auntie couldn't simply be an evil witch chasing them. But that didn't mean she was going to allow herself to be caught.

Auntie clambered out of her chair and stretched her arms over the entrance, blocking Yeo-deol's path to the door. Up close like this, Yeo-deol smelled pine and wet dirt. Up close like this, she saw the fear of a cornered animal in the quivering downward tilt of Auntie's chin.

"I helped you last night; I let you see into my humiliation," Auntie whispered, her fingernails pressing into the wooden frames. "Don't you want to see what's going on?"

"I didn't need your help. We were all fine before you arrived, before Mama disappeared." Yeo-deol clutched her spinning head. "But Mama came and you left. No, Mama left and you came."

In the holes of her memories, Mama and Auntie blurred together without a distinctive beginning or ending. Auntie in a straw hat under the summer sun squatting down beside Yeo-deol with a fresh apple. Mama leaning over Yeo-deol in the darkened turret, tucking in the blanket with a grim determination. Auntie rocking a wailing Yeol as Yeo-deol and the other girls stood on their toes for a peek. Mama shoving away Daddy in the gallery and the clench of his jaw.

"Stop it!"

Auntie was violating her memory, like how she had washed her tears into Yeo-deol.

"Stay out of my body, and stay out of my head," Yeo-deol said, pushing past Auntie, whose lips were forming around a denial. *It wasn't me*, Mama's voice fanned over her as Auntie crashed to the floor. Not daring to look back, Yeo-deol ran down the length of the hallway, panting to outrun the flood of false memories.

CHAPTER 11

The faint light of the foyer washing over Yeo-deol was a beacon of safety. She had sprinted the whole length of the hallway, uncertain if the footsteps behind her were echoes of herself or Auntie pursuing her.

The silence of the foyer settled over Yeo-deol oddly. She looked around the floor for her sisters and spotted the familiar ebony trunk, painted in teal accents and red flowers, in the center of the foyer. The top was flung open, meaning her sisters had already passed through for their new dresses.

Mama usually sent out the clothes trunk when Daddy was holding one of his big dinner parties. The girls antici-pated its return because they never knew what would emerge from the black trunk. One year, it had been gray chiffon gowns, chill to the touch. Yeo-deol had loved dipping her fin-gers in the material. More recently, in the autumn, Mama had dressed them in the burnished colors of acidic fruits: blue plum, lemon, grapefruit, apple, peach, orange, lime, mango, pomegranate, grape.

"My, my, all these lovely fruits to pick from," Daddy's friends had joked.

A red-orange dress was draped across the trunk. The crimped satin bodice resembled a seashell freshly plucked out of the water. It was Hana's dress, based on the red ribbon tied around the hanger. All the girls likewise had their own colored ribbon that Mama used to distinguish their dresses. Yeo-deol's ribbon was lavender.

There was a rustling behind Yeo-deol on the stairs, faint enough that she might have imagined it. In a sense of déjà vu, she approached the base of the stairs, assuring herself that in the day, there was an order and reason to the things that happened.

Nothing could have braced Yeo-deol for the sight before her.

Only one girl registered at a time, sprawled along the steps. Some were lying down and others were slumped forward. Their distinctive hair color, not quite black like Mama's or brown like Daddy's, swam into their faces, obscuring who was whom. Yeo-deol's legs gave out from under her.

"Dul?"

"Set?"

"Net?"

"Da-seot?"

"Yeo-seot?"

"Il-gop?"

"Ahop?"

"Yeol?"

Yeo-deol called out for each of her sisters, but there was no response.

Knowing she needed to call to Daddy, the maids, anybody, even Auntie, Yeo-deol pounded a fist to her chest to dislodge the scream burning up her throat.

My sisters...

My sisters...

My sisters...

Under the flat of her hand, the ground quaked.

The house, it felt her pain, it was mourning with her.

Yeo-deol kneeled onto the floor, pressing her forehead into the convulsions. It would be so easy to dig beneath the foundation of the house and rip it out, like pulling a tree out by its roots. She would form the hand in her mind that reached into the ground. She would demolish this house because this house was nothing without her sisters.

"I told you guys this isn't funny—"

"Shit, shit, she's losing her head, do you see that? Get up, get up."

Yeo-deol raised her head.

Set sat up in a mint dress glinting like subtle dew, followed by Dul, whose silver harness corset fitted over a blue organza gown gave her the appearance of a war heroine, a cowardly one who played dead in battles. The quaking died away.

Her sisters popped up one by one, their faces stricken. Net had a look resembling guilt in her pursed mouth, fidgeting with her pink tulle dress that bloomed into a cascade of flowers. Last of all, Il-gop sat up in the brash outline of a violet pleated dress, a melding of raven feathers, that matched the defiant temper scrunched into her forehead.

Il-gop had been holding the littles, Ahop and Yeol, during the act. The two littles blinked at Yeo-deol with matching blank expressions, as if they had been startled out of their natural dispositions. Ahop wore a white webbed gown of lace that seemed to cage her in; meanwhile, Yeol had a more docile look in the voluminous puff of a red skirt.

The hues and forms of her sisters' new dresses blurred in Yeo-deol's tears.

"It was supposed to be funny." Il-gop glared at Yeo-deol.

"How were we supposed to know you were going to go all mental and try to dig a hole in the ground? I guess we forgot that you're a little damaged in the head now. It'd happen to anyone after falling down three stories," Il-gop finished in the cheery affect she used with Daddy, pretending she had not intentionally invoked a taboo memory.

Dul ran a hand over her shaved head, but she said nothing.

"I hope you all really drop dead," Yeo-deol said.

At the same time, the relief coursed new air through her lungs. No one commented about the quaking, and Yeo-deol sensed that they had been oblivious to it like the cracking windows in the dining room.

Da-seot floated down the stairs in a champagne tulle gown patterned in flowers. This sweet personification of spring rushed into Yeo-deol's arms, kicking up the layers of her skirt that seemed to float up real flowers.

Sincere remorse sloped down Da-seot's brows. She looked placeless in the space without Hana in front to lead and command her.

"We heard you coming, and Il-gop said it would make you laugh. I thought it would make you laugh," Da-seot said, bringing Yeo-deol into a tight hug. She let herself be held like this, admiring the symmetry of Da-seot's face.

"I'm sorry, I'm sorry, I'm sorry," Da-seot whispered into Yeo-deol's hair.

What seemed to be an overwrought apology turned into a graceful incantation, nine times. Yeo-deol realized Da-seot was speaking an apology for each sister who remained tight-lipped behind them on the stairs, choked up by pride or lack of courage.

Taking in the collective view of her sisters over Da-seot's shoulders, Yeo-deol could see that Mama had outdone herself this time. The dresses had been cut out of the fabric of their ordinary personalities and made beautiful by Mama's magic. Even Yeo-seot, who gnawed at her nails in hunger, was cast in a sorrowful dignity by the deep green of her satin gown.

Da-seot finished her incantation with a kiss on Yeo-deol's forehead.

As she was being pulled toward the clothes trunk, Yeo-deol hoped Da-seot would outgrow their domineering eldest sister one day.

At the trunk, Da-seot picked up Hana's gown so that Yeo-deol could reach in for her dress. She pulled out a yellow square of folded fabric, inconceivably small compared to the grandeur and dimension of the dresses her sisters wore. The unmistakable lavender ribbon wrapped around the yellow square marked it as hers, though.

Yeo-deol untied the ribbon and unfolded the square.

There was no dramatic roll out of a long skirt, no surprise like a dress that continued to unfold on itself that made it make sense. In her hands, Yeo-deol held a worn, yellow button-up shirt. It was the kind that Daddy wore with his suits and ties.

"There must have been a mistake," Da-seot insisted, peering into the empty trunk that remained empty. The rustle of her spring dress was mocking to Yeo-deol's ears.

Yeo-deol stared at the lavender ribbon discarded by her foot and shook her head.

For some reason, Mama had given all the girls beautiful dresses, except for Yeo-deol. She had not been deemed worthy in Mama's eyes.

Hugging the yellow shirt in her arms, Yeo-deol hurried into the hallway, escaping eight pairs of pitying eyes.

She didn't need their pity; that was but a flimsy cover for the relief that it hadn't been one of them. The competition had naturally started whenever Mama or Daddy hesitated over their names or were missing exactly one of something, forcing a choice: Out of the ten girls, who would slip through the cracks of Mama and Daddy's minds?

I like my shirt because Mama chose it for me, Yeo-deol repeated to herself.

Still, the faded yellow of the shirt couldn't compare to the yellow wrapping paper of Auntie's gifts, the yellow boxes that had smelled of both rot and sweetness in her dreams.

Yeo-deol headed to the kitchen, feeling the pantry key warming in the heel of her right shoe. Inside the kitchen, the maids didn't acknowledge the slight parting of the curtain of herbs by Yeo-deol crouched on the ground. There were fewer of them, perhaps five or so sloped against the tables and counters, compared to the usual fifteen or twenty of them bustling around. They looked so pale and drained of energy. Maybe Daddy had misjudged the cause of Hana's sickness.

A kettle whistled, breaking Yeo-deol's ruminations.

She hurriedly unlocked the pantry door before any of the maids might notice, and crawled into the dark hole. Her forehead pushed into something cold and smooth, something human. An expanse of forehead. The smell of pine and wet dirt. Hazel eyes.

"Please," Auntie whispered, "I'm hiding from your daddy."

Brittle crumbs dug into Yeo-deol's palms on the floor, a reminder of the poisoned pastries Mama used to serve Daddy's friends, and Daddy himself, with a smile. Yeo-deol didn't want to leave the pantry either, thinking of her sisters, who were probably twirling around in their beautiful dresses and pitying their forgotten eighth sister.

"How did you get in here?" Yeo-deol asked, pressing down on the heel of her right shoe to confirm that she had put the key back.

"I'm not sure. I wanted a dark space to hide in and I ended up here. I didn't know that there was a door until you came through it." Auntie struggled through her explanation, like she was piecing it together for herself.

Yeo-deol didn't trust Auntie, yet she could believe her distress. The process sounded similar to the pictures that Yeo-deol had been able to create in her mind since falling from the balcony, except more powerful. Auntie was essentially willing into reality what she desired and admitting this openly to Yeo-deol.

"I'll scream if you do anything weird," Yeo-deol relented.

In a way, she too didn't want Auntie to become trapped by Daddy. *Because I want to preserve my own family*, Yeo-deol rationalized. She couldn't unpack either Auntie's fear of Daddy or Mama's secret agenda against him yet.

"Thank you," Auntie said.

The two of them sat facing each other in the cramped darkness. Each movement and breath touched the other, an intimacy that should have been suffocating with this woman who was encroaching into their family and home, their memories, and Mama's seat. Instead, Yeo-deol felt secure in this stale air sanctified by Mama's silent contempt, a carefully tended contempt that had never extended to the girls and would protect her now.

"Since I'm letting you stay, tell me a story to pass the time," Yeo-deol said.

"Please," she added in an afterthought, catching Hana's tone in her command.

"I don't know any stories, though," Auntie said.

"Not even anything your mama or daddy read to you?"

"I don't have a mama or daddy."

Yeo-deol nodded knowingly. In the books that Mama read to her and her sisters, such characters without a mama or daddy were called orphans, and they led spectacular lives, discovering better families or journeying to new worlds. In some books, the characters escaped their parents and lived as temporary orphans, abounding in freedom and magic that the adults didn't believe in and therefore couldn't experience. It made sense to Yeo-deol that Auntie was one of these orphans.

"Tell me about your life without a mama or daddy as a story then, from the beginning, or else I'll throw you out of the pantry," Yeo-deol said in half-hearted menace.

She wanted to spend away as much of this humiliating day as she could in this dark hole and put it behind her.

There was silence. Auntie's hazel eyes dimmed, like they had during breakfast, and Yeo-deol saw her reflection becoming blotted out.

"In the beginning, I woke up in snow. It was so cold."

White puffs of air spilled from Auntie's mouth.

Yeo-deol tensed but stayed quiet, not wanting to spook Auntie sitting in this snowy beginning, removed from the pantry.

"All I could see in the darkness was a teal shape in the distance. The teal turned into the roof of the glass turret, and I could see you and your sisters inside. You looked so warm that I followed the turret, and I arrived at your house."

"You lied then, what you said the first time about wanting to meet us for a long time," Yeo-deol said.

Auntie shook her head, dispersing melting flakes of snow on Yeo-deol's hand.

"I walked for a long time. I walked long enough to see the sun go out and become relit by a giant ball of gas. I walked long enough to catch up to my body. I walked long enough to know you one by one, filling up my heart painfully. I walked until the darkness turned into a forest."

We filled up Auntie's heart, Yeo-deol thought, burrowing a finger into the dirt ground.

If Auntie hadn't left so abruptly, if she had stayed after Yeo-deol's plummet and comforted her sisters, if Yeo-deol had woken up to find her, they might have accepted her eventually. They might have eventually believed that she, in fact, was their Mama. But she had left, disappearing on them like Mama.

Yeo-deol startled at a drop of water on her shoulder, and then another.

"When I thought you died, I ran back into the darkness. I continued to run even when you woke up because I wanted to lie down and go back to nothing. I lay in the snow and waited, but my heart unraveled with your sadness. It was unbearable."

A drop of water ran down Yeo-deol's cheek into her mouth, tasting of salt.

"So I decided to come back with presents for my girls, to cheer you up out of your misery," Auntie said brightly.

The drizzle of her tears thickened in the pantry.

To cheer you up out of your misery. The words knocked into Yeo-deol's chest.

Yeo-deol woke up to a bobbing motion like a small boat in a gentle ocean.

Auntie was carrying her up the stairs. The sleepless night had caught up to Yeo-deol in the pantry. "Don't," Yeo-deol had whispered to Auntie before she drifted off.

Don't disturb anything of mine.

Don't cry.

Don't leave.

It was night already out the windows they passed. Lunch and dinner had somehow slipped by them. Auntie had buttoned up Yeo-deol into the yellow shirt, her nightgown underneath still damp from the tears inside the pantry.

Yeo-deol squirmed on Auntie's back to indicate she wanted off.

"It's okay," Auntie said. "I made it this far, I can reach the end."

"Okay," Yeo-deol breathed, only because her eyes were growing heavy again.

"Why do you girls live so high up?" Auntie panted under her.

"Mama told us that if the house ever crumbled apart in the night, the turret would be the last thing to hit the ground. And we would see the sky the whole time," Yeo-deol whispered.

"But what if the house crumbles from the top?" Auntie's arms around Yeo-deol slackened. Yeo-deol gripped her hands tighter at the base of Auntie's neck.

"Then that means my sisters and I will die first," Yeo-deol said.

She closed her eyes to a tiredness that wasn't hers, preceding her from a faraway yet close place and time. The tiredness flowed through her veins, shrouding Yeo-deol's eyes and ears, like the wave of drowsiness that had led her to Mama. Her breath rattled in her chest.

What do you desire the most in your heart? a voice, a thought, a dream asked her.

It was Santa's beard tickling her ear. It was a blank page fluttering down from the air. It was the witch's white coat brushing her cheek.

I want to remember.

I want to remember what my real Mama looks like.

Yeo-deol ebbed away to nothing.

CHAPTER 12

───

Dugun… Dugun… Dugun…

Yeo-deol opened her eyes. The tips of tall grass pricked into a black sky fresh with stars. It was as if she had woken up from a nap while leisurely stargazing. The mild night quickly lost its charm, however. Yeo-deol stood up and found that the towering grass blocked any visibility. When she chose a direction and began to set out, her feet didn't budge. The mud underfoot she had sunken into had hardened around her shoes.

Yeo-deol sighed.

Leaving her shoes behind, she skipped over the mud blindly, hoping there would be an eventual end to the field, as well as this dream. She had learned from the mounds on the island that it wouldn't be as simple as going back to sleep.

The dream had a will and a way, which seemed to come down to pushing forward until something gave.

As if to prove her point, the ground under her bare feet solidified into an upward slope. Yeo-deol climbed up the embankment that flattened to a road that appeared newly paved by its smoothness. The whole area was an endless stretch of the road, bordered by the black loom of nearby mountains. Yeo-deol scooted off the road for safety, even though there were no cars or signs of life. Hugging her legs to herself, she waited for what would come down the road.

A shriek of laugher split open the quiet.

Yeo-deol squinted in the distance at the two figures that had materialized on the road. Drawing closer in lurched steps, Mama stepped out of the darkness, hand in hand with the man from the yellow house on stilts, Dong-ju. They had changed their clothes, Mama in high-waisted plaid pants and a red top, and Dong-ju, who looked more modest in brown pants and a white shirt.

They were no longer connected by their hands, instead freely shoving and collapsing into each other. Their disjointed movements converged together by the touch of their shoulders or the sliding clasp of their hands.

The ground under Yeo-deol rumbled as an army truck sped down the road, gaining on the drunken couple rapidly. Mama and Dong-ju had time to escape, but they carried on in their swaying path, apparently deaf to the increasing drone of the truck's engine.

"Mama!" Yeo-deol pulled at her legs, which had become rooted to where she stood.

The dream wasn't allowing her to intervene. She was being forced to watch.

"Mama!" The scream lashed up her throat and exploded over the roar of the truck. In the cone of light, the silhouette of Mama's head turned too late. The truck barreled into Mama and Dong-ju soundlessly.

Yeo-deol stared enraptured at the two bodies bounding into the air. They landed at her feet, exactly where the dream had wanted her to be, but her eyes fixed on the airborne arc of the truck that whipped up her hair. The dip of the empty front cab—*Nobody is driving the truck*—the feminine shrieks and yells pitching from the covered truck bed—*Where were they going?*

There was a tapping at Yeo-deol's ankle, almost politely.

"Did you fall out of the truck?" Mama asked in Korean, her words somehow coming out clearly through the twisted protrusion of her lips. Mama's cheekbone was smashed into the pavement, throwing her features in a swollen slant like a piece of dropped dough.

Yeo-deol bent down and dumbly nodded the wrong answer to Mama's question.

Her bare feet warmed in the blood that trickled from Mama's hairline and washed her face red, a stark contrast to the white of the single eye on Yeo-deol.

"Did you see my mother inside the truck? She has really black hair but hazel eyes. Pretty."

There was a blank in Yeo-deol's mind for the grandmother she had never seen.

"N-No? It's…um…it's too dark inside," Yeo-deol stammered, feeling the need to keep up the pretension now.

"Oh, well, it's probably a different truck. I'm glad you're out, though. When I'm lying here waiting to die, I tell myself that next time I'll stop the truck. Maybe none of you inside want that and you'll be annoyed with me. I just want to make sure before the truck continues on. But then it loops back to the beginning, and I always become distracted."

Mama's eye rotated to Dong-ju, face down in a spreading pool of blood. Like a painting of symmetry, Dong-ju lay at Yeo-deol's left foot and Mama at her right foot, their limp hands reaching toward each other.

"It's funny. He's usually wearing his yellow shirt, but this time, it was like someone plucked his shirt off his back. And then you appear in a yellow shirt! If I didn't know Dong-ju better, I'd be jealous."

Yeo-deol had no idea how to make sense of what Mama was saying. For all she knew, this was the nonsense rambling of a person facing death. Yet, faced with her own Mama bleeding out to death, Yeo-deol decided it was worth tracing out the meaning.

Already, the blood on Mama's face was drying to a more languid trickle.

"Where were you coming from? You must have walked for a long time," Yeo-deol said, unable to fathom the beginning of this seemingly endless road.

"I'm coming from a party. I'm Dong-ju's prize for the night, or maybe he's my prize. I wish I'm not as drunk, but the loop always begins on this road, after the party. That's Dong-ju, by the way." Mama rotated her single eye back to Dong-ju.

Yeo-deol awkwardly raised a hand up in greeting to Dong-ju, who remained facedown. Feeling disrespectful, she lowered her hand. Mama seemed to appreciate the gesture, though, and laughed at the interaction.

"If it's a loop, does that mean this happens again and again?" Yeo-deol asked.

"Yep. Dong-ju and I walk for a little while, the truck comes and hits us, he dies first, and then I die, finally. The dying part hurts a bit, there's a swarming sort of darkness for a while, and then Dong-ju and I will be back there again, where we came from on the road."

It sounded like an exhausting cycle, a pointless one that didn't need to go on.

"If you always know the truck is coming, you could avoid it and wait for it to pass," Yeo-deol said, trying to tamp down the frustration at seeing her Mama like this.

"Don't look at me like that, like you want to cry. I learned a long time ago that the trucks will keep coming until we die. Dong-ju doesn't understand because he forgets every time we loop back. Besides, there's so many other things I want to talk to him about."

Mama's single eye was drooping closed.

Yeo-deol held out a finger under Mama's nostril and to her relief, felt faint breathing. She had one more question to ask this Mama stuck in a hellish limbo of dying over and over again.

"Do you think you could ever kill Dong-ju?" Yeo-deol asked, leaning in for the answer. If it all connected together, the agonized man trapped inside Mama's teal telephone in Dul's dream was Dong-ju.

Perhaps it was obvious what this Mama would answer, but Yeo-deol wanted to hear the obvious answer from any Mama's mouth.

"Maybe, yeah. Not intentionally." Mama heaved to reach the end of her sentence for Yeo-deol.

"I think if we were split apart, we could kill each other slowly. We could go on with our lives on the outside, but on the inside, we'd become twisted, cracked versions of ourselves, never smooth or whole like we were together."

"You shouldn't tie yourself to one person like that," Yeo-deol bit out harshly, trying to rub the tears back into her eyes. She was sick of crying, yet it ached so deeply, thinking for how long Mama, her real Mama, had kept this pain to herself.

"Right, you really shouldn't." Mama halted mid-laughter.

Finding no words sufficient to send this Mama off, Yeo-deol sat numbly in the pool of blood. She didn't know what to do or where she was supposed to go next.

Yeo-deol squeaked when Mama raised her arm and haltingly waved her over. "Where are your shoes?" she asked, her voice a mere wisp.

"They got stuck in the mud," Yeo-deol answered and then belatedly recalled that she was supposed to have fallen from the truck.

"Take my shoes. It's a gift. I hope when the loop starts again, you won't be here."

Yeo-deol looked down at her bare feet.

In Mama's own words, the loop would reset everything, meaning the women in the truck would always come. Whether she was wishing the girl from the truck a miracle or had discerned a difference, Yeo-deol obeyed, even though slipping the white sneakers off Mama's feet thrilled her with unspeakable irreverence.

The sneakers fit Yeo-deol's feet perfectly, and she didn't question it. A little way down the road, a pink-painted door had appeared. It was time for her to go. Yeo-deol pressed a kiss to Mama's forehead. Flecks of her blood stuck to her lips.

"Thank you for the shoes."

Wearing her new shoes, Yeo-deol ran down the road toward the door in powerful strides. When she looked back, Mama and Dong-ju and their pool of blood were gone. Somewhere, they were waking up and starting down the same road. Yeo-deol hastened through the pink door, knowing she couldn't bear to see Mama die for a second time.

Dugun... Dugun... Dugun...

Of course, the pink door led into the pink room.

The lace curtains lifted in a soothing breeze as Yeo-deol closed the door softly. The blood soaked into her yellow shirt and white sneakers had faded to a shadow.

"There you are. I've been waiting for you," Mama said, this time in English.

Underneath the wrought-iron chandelier hanging with the tinfoil stars, a colorless Mama turned around to face Yeo-deol. In her arms, she held a blanket bundled in her arms. The absence of any hue blanched her tidy hair and the gown flowing into a train that consumed the floor.

"Would you like to meet your ninth sister?" Mama asked, looking at Yeo-deol clearly, unlike the Mama in the yellow house on stilts or the Mama in the loop.

Yeo-deol nodded and drew closer, stiffened in awe by this colorless Mama's regality. The air seemed to be suspended around her, as if taking care in its breath too.

Lifting onto her toes, Yeo-deol peered into the bundle and blinked.

Gray eyes plucked out from Daddy. A tuft of black hair. The baby that stared back at Yeo-deol wasn't her sister, Ahop. Tinkling laugher erupted from the small mouth in chiming dollops that dropped into Yeo-deol's ears like precious pearls.

"Her name is *Gippeum*. It means happiness," Mama said.

The laugher continued to rise in a volume panging into Yeo-deol's eardrums. It was punishing her, as if Yeo-deol had already been deemed unworthy of happiness.

Yeo-deol looked up at Mama in bewilderment.

Mama's chin quivered. The black chasms of her eyes seemed to dilate with the pain expanding inside her as she lay a hand over the baby's face, silencing the terrible sound. When she withdrew her hand, the baby's face had seeped into a gray pallor, freezing the tiny lips in the shape of phantom laughter.

"It's my fault. I thought this time I could pour all my happiness into a new girl. I thought I could give my girls happiness," Mama said, her cheeks glinting with jeweled tears.

Desperate to console her forlorn Mama, Yeo-deol surrendered to the bow of her body that was moving of its own volition to kiss the ninth sister that she had never been able to meet. When Yeo-deol pulled away, the flakes of dried blood she had carried over from the Mama in the loop stuck to the baby's forehead.

"Thank you," Mama said, although Yeo-deol didn't know what she had done, exactly.

Mama unwrapped the blanket around the baby and nestled it around Yeo-deol's shoulders. Yeo-deol tried to protest, but Mama shook her head.

"It's a gift. This is the blanket I wrapped you girls in as I created each of you. But no more...no more," she said, touching the small gray hand.

Mama lowered her head over the baby.

Feeling the dream quieting to an end, Yeo-deol slowly backed away, gripping the blanket around her shoulders. From the chandelier hung the eleven stars she had counted over and over again when confined alone in the pink room. Eleven girls; there had been eleven of them in all.

The room began to darken around the edges, swallowing Mama with it.

Five of the stars dropped to the ground, their frayed strings from the chandelier dumbly floating in the shock of violence. Yeo-deol broke into a run out the door, knowing something must have happened to her sisters.

Dugun... Dugun... Dugun...

Yeo-deol's feet pounded up the winding stairs leading to the glass turret. In her new sneakers that seemed to add a spring to each step, she reached the turret faster than she ever had. Under the lavender sky spread over the glass, Yeo-deol passed nine lumps of blankets, too scared to check under them. She would check on her real sisters once she woke up.

At her pillow, there was a yellow box wrapped with a pink ribbon, her gift from Auntie. *A gift to cheer me out of my misery,* a voice in Yeo-deol echoed.

She began to reach for the ribbon, reasoning that it wouldn't take very long, that finding out what was inside could help make up her mind decisively toward Auntie. A puff of air interrupted Yeo-deol, and she looked up to see the blanket lumps deflating down the line, heading toward her. Shoving aside the gift, Yeo-deol threw her own blanket over her head and squeezed her eyes closed.

CHAPTER 13

———

The blanket swarmed over Yeo-deol's head in undulating waves. It was Auntie, pressing her hands in to probe for what she wanted. It was Mama, rousing Yeo-deol to tell her she had come back. It was Dr. Roberts, come to take her to see the circus, far away from this house.

"Everything is crumbling apart," a choked whisper tickled into her ear as the blanket was ripped away.

Yeo-deol's hands fanned open in surrender. Da-seot, Yeo-seot, and Il-gop stood over her with stunned expressions, holding the twisted length of the blanket in their hands. The black night sky through the turret glass confirmed she had exited the layered dream, finally. Her relief was cut short by Il-gop closing in. Her delicate violin-playing hands, the hands that she so vigilantly protected, came down on Yeo-deol in unrelenting punches.

"I thought you died in there," her hot breath fanned over Yeo-deol.

Under the blows of Il-gop's pinkening knuckles, Yeo-deol could only manage to protect her head, slack in bewilderment. At least Dul's aggressions had a meticulous hand that doled out pain in a relished torture, which Yeo-deol had learned to endure. Il-gop beat down without restraint, having surpassed the point of seeing Yeo-deol sputtering and heaving for breath under her. She would kill Yeo-deol eventually.

I thought you died in there. A hypothetical grief had unscrewed her formidable sister, and Yeo-deol didn't know whose liquid black eyes looked down on her. There was no familiar sister inside those eyes to which she could appeal, and as the tempo undulated between abusive lashings of anger and dense knockings of sorrow, it was as if the two of them switched from oppressor to oppressed, subjugator to subjugated, one enemy line to another.

A tiredness, an anger, a burden that preceded all of them.

For how much longer do I have to suffer like this? Yeo-deol thought in an exhale of pain. What was it about her that made her cruelest sisters pick her out and inflict their violence?

"Stop, Il-gop, please stop," Da-seot screamed behind them uselessly.

Yeo-seot interrupted the fight with a shove that toppled Il-gop. As Yeo-deol was helped up into a sitting position, she worried, seeing her sixth sister's sunken contours and the sharpened jut of her elbows. The hunger was no longer about food. Yeo-seot continued to lose weight day by day, wasting away to a consuming hunger she didn't try to fill anymore. Yeo-deol couldn't fathom how those bony arms had summoned the force to overpower Il-gop just now.

"Dul, Set, and Net are gone, like Hana," Yeo-seot stated.

Yeo-deol looked to the elders girls' empty sleeping spaces. Their blankets were turned out and pulled out on the floor, as if they had left in a hurry. The remaining girls were clustered around Yeo-deol. The littles, Ahop and Yeol, were asleep under a shared blanket in Il-gop's usual sleeping spot next to Yeo-deol. This was a formation of crisis around her.

"We didn't know you were in the turret, so we assumed you had disappeared until we saw your blanket lump. But the blanket wouldn't lift up, like it was glued down," Da-seot explained.

"Auntie carried me up to the turret," Yeo-deol said, recalling the hazy ascent up the stairway. "Did you see her today?"

The frantic communication that ensued in the eyes of Da-seot, Yeo-seot, and Il-gop was sufficient answer for Yeo-deol, their hesitation only meaning they wanted to hide something.

"I'm sorry," Da-seot blurted, her honest eyes twinging with guilt, "We should have waited for you, but we opened the yellow boxes Auntie brought for us after dinner."

"Only because the witch kept on insisting," Il-gop said.

"Auntie told us she had chosen the gifts out specially with Mama, like our new dresses," Yeo-seot said, her flitting eyes gauging Yeo-deol's reaction.

Hearing Mama and Auntie in the same sentence, put together in the same breath of space, felt like a dissonant impossibility. It contradicted the Auntie with whom she had sat together in Mama's pantry, who had told Yeo-deol how she had been born in the snow and attempted to return to it before she came back to the girls.

"What was inside your boxes?" Yeo-deol asked warily.

"What we desired most in our hearts," Da-seot answered, wiggling her toes as her cheeks glowed with pleasure. Neither Yeo-seot nor Il-gop volunteered what had been inside their boxes as well, but their faces seemed to soften, picturing what they had received. Her sisters' inner-most desires were private, and Yeo-deol understood she couldn't force them to answer.

A bleary question from the ascent up the stairs came back to Yeo-deol.

What do you desire most in your heart?

Yeo-deol's heart stuttered faster. *Dugun...Dugun...Dugun.*

"Auntie will let you open yours tomorrow," Yeo-seot said with a quiet certainty, trying to comfort her. But Auntie had already delivered Yeo-deol's yellow box in her dream. It had only been a matter of bad timing that Yeo-deol didn't get to open it.

"No, we need to get rid of these gifts. I think they have to do with why Dul, Set, and Net are gone," Yeo-deol said, rising to her feet urgently. She bumped into Da-seot, Yeo-seot, and Il-gop, who had formed a wall with their bodies.

"What?" Da-seot asked, her eyes glinting oddly. "How can we just throw out what we desired most in our hearts now that we have it?"

"I need mine," Yeo-seot said, twisting her hands together.

"I'll kill you before you take away mine," Il-gop glowered.

"I thought we didn't trust Auntie. Gifts don't just come for free, and we can't hate Auntie but accept her gifts," Yeo-deol said, finding it difficult to pin down her uneasiness.

She looked down at her feet to the white sneakers from the Mama in the loop. They had solidly stayed despite awakening from the dream. Yeo-deol hadn't questioned accepting the shoes as a gift because it had been from Mama, even if not her exact Mama. "Where are your shoes?" she had asked in such a Mama-like tone, noticing Yeo-deol's bare feet even as she bled out to death on a highway.

Dr. Roberts had also given her strange, beautiful gifts, and while she didn't know what to make of him, the meaning behind his gifts had been straightforward enough: a deadly pen to protect herself, pink earmuffs to protect her ears, a promise in the form of circus animal-shaped chocolates. In comparison, the cold cunning to Auntie's perfect yellow boxes struck Yeo-deol. Auntie had already disarmed and ensnared her sisters with what they wanted most.

"In the books Mama reads to us, the evil witch gives first because she wants something back," Yeo-deol said in a final attempt to reason with her sisters.

She looked back up to an empty turret. Da-seot, Yeo-seot, Il-gop, and even the sleeping littles, Ahop and Yeol, were gone, and in their spots gleamed tinfoil stars, five in all. Auntie had taken all her sisters. Blurred by loss, Yeo-deol didn't know what else to do but circle the glass turret, crying bitterly as she walked along her sisters' blankets that smelled of must and shampoo.

Daddy will know what to do, she thought as she deposited all the dream Mamas' gifts into a makeshift sack made out of her pillowcase: the blanket from the colorless Mama that surfaced under her bigger blanket, and the sun-browned Mama's underwear that had remained in her nightgown pocket. With some hesitation, Yeo-deol added Dr. Roberts's pen that she had been hiding under her sleeping mat.

Down the winding stairs, the pain of Yeo-deol's uneven steps should have been anchoring enough that she was awake, but the black sky she had taken as a dependable sign had become overcast. The passage was submerged in lavender light from the windows, and Yeo-deol couldn't tell anymore if this was a dream or her reality pitched into a nightmare.

Clamping her palm between her teeth, Yeo-deol bit down until she drew blood, not knowing how much pain really distinguished dreams from living.

Dugun... Dugun... Dugun...

The house had become strange to Yeo-deol. In the shadowed hallways, the familiar shapes—a grandfather clock, vases, pillars—all seemed misplaced. Yeo-deol committed to the direction with the least lavender light and ran down the length of the corridor.

The corridor ended in a room, from which an orange glow emitted. Yeo-deol entered the room, wielding the pen tip in front of her. The dining room had been reordered. All the chairs at the table were lined up on one side of the table facing Yeo-deol. Her sisters sat with their heads bowed to their plates. In the middle sat a naked Mama, whose glazed look impressed a deadness from her body and this present place. Could this be her real Mama?

Yeo-deol averted her eyes, embarrassed to stare any longer at Mama's nakedness.

The spacing of the sitting arrangement tugged at Yeo-deol's memory.

The five sisters on Mama's left side were clustered together in one group, their shoulders touching into each other, and the other four sisters on Mama's right side formed another group. There was an empty chair on the right side for Yeo-deol. Mama's seat in the middle was set apart by its lonesome, yet the bowed heads on either sides were all angled toward her.

The pictures about someone else's divine love, Yeo-deol remembered.

They were arranged in the dinner scene from the tapestry of Biblical scenes. "That one's called *The Last Supper*," Daddy had said. Except now the picture had manifested into their last supper with the hellish twist of her sisters' bowed heads. Yeo-deol had no way of discerning who was whom. Their dark hair swam out from their plates, as if they had fallen asleep into their food.

Yeo-deol broke into laugher, understanding what this was about.

"Hahahahahaha."

She had learned from the other day in the foyer. If she laughed, if she acknowledged the prank was funny, her sisters would get up from their game of playing dead.

"Hahahahahahahahahahaha."

Her sisters didn't stir though, not one bit.

"Hahahahahahaahahaahahahahahaha."

Her sisters didn't get up, not one peep.

A sweat broke over Yeo-deol's forehead as she hurried up to the table and shook her sisters one by one, who all slackened back down lifelessly. In front of each girl was a second set of plates containing disparate items. Some belonged on a table, like a stone pot of *bibimbap* filled with steaming rice and vegetables, a warm bottle of milk, and Korean honey cookies. The other items were more difficult to understand on a plate: a heaping of light, a square of blue stained glass, a compact vault, red shoes, and a silver pitch pipe.

The most grotesque object lay before the first girl, a face hollowed in the eyes and mouth. By the red jagged edges of the skin, it seemed to have been directly cut out from a person. A similar, yet different mask came back to Yeo-deol's mind forcefully. The mask had floated in the water she had looked down upon from the height of the yellow house on stilts. In the moment, she had denied who immediately came to mind in the bulb of the bridgeless nose, the lost distance between the eyes, the thin lips that seemed pursed in a command. *It couldn't be*, Yeo-deol had thought, because she hadn't wanted it to be true. But Hana hadn't been there in the morning.

The face laid out on the plate was smoothed out from the mask she had seen in the water, with a sculptured rise of the nose, softly placed eye hollows, and plush lips, ready to be worn. It resembled Da-seot, and if worn properly on the face, could surpass their most beautiful sister. This was the face that Hana must have always wanted, the desire that manifested in her tyranny over Da-seot. This must have been what Hana desired the most in her heart: a new face.

The items that sat before her each of sisters on the plates was their last supper. Auntie had killed her sisters with what they desired the most, and in the middle, Mama was dead to what was going on. Yeo-deol knew she needed to go find and save Daddy. She needed to go, but her legs had lost the will to hold her up.

"I've been waiting for you."

Yeo-deol froze and slowly lifted her head.

Net sat up in her chair with her arms possessively snaked around the safe on her plate. Her irises had clouded into a milky white, and the blue pallor of her skin looked fragile in the fractured web of purple veins. Net's blinks were sluggish under the twinkling frost in her eyelashes and peppering down her stiffened hair.

"Net, what are you…how are you…are you…?"

Yeo-deol struggled to form a coherent sentence through her shock and the sudden spike of hope that perhaps she hadn't shaken her sisters hard enough.

"You broke my heart," Net's voice drooped flatly. "You shoved me away although I loved you. The shards pierced me here," she pointed to her rib, "here," she pointed to the base of her throat, "here," she pointed to the curve of her earlobe, "and here," she pointed to her chest.

The faint memory of pulling free from Net's grasp in the turret stirred inside of Yeo-deol, settling into guilt as she saw Net falling backward out of sight. But Yeo-deol had been trying to save Dul from becoming erased. How could loving one sister come down to losing another?

"I'm sorry for pushing you," Yeo-deol said, because she was truly sorry for that.

"I loved you, you were mine, and I was yours. You broke my heart," Net slurred.

"You shouldn't tie yourself to one person like that," Yeo-deol said, echoing back what she had told the Mama trapped in the loop.

There was no way to know if Net understood because her head crashed back into her plate. Yeo-deol began to step toward the table, but stopped, wide-eyed. The mass of her sisters' dark hair was elongating down the table and surging toward her in a towering wave.

Yeo-deol flew out of the room, her pillowcase swinging out behind her.

"Daddy!" Yeo-deol screamed down the hallway.

Dugun... Dugun... Dugun...

Her shoulder collided into a door, which caved in with impossible ease. The slither of hair wasn't far behind her, dogged in its chase. Yeo-deol stared at the gouge she had created in the wood and tested the surface of several more doors. It seemed the material of the doors had become unstable, almost malleable, like the rest of the house.

Hearing the slither of hair drawing close and knowing she couldn't run for much longer, Yeo-deol beat down the line of doors, puncturing small holes that let her see into the rooms and allowed her to check for Daddy efficiently. The wood still splintered into Yeo-deol's hands painfully, though, reminding her that she was in a confused place between waking and not waking. She looked into a yellow room humming nursery rhymes, several darkened rooms, a room of a battlefield littered with soldiers, but none of them contained Daddy.

An explosion of dust from a hole caught Yeo-deol into a choke. Coughing over the settling dust, Yeo-deol looked inside and saw Daddy sitting at his desk. The tendrils of hair were beginning to creep up her ankle as she closed the door of the study behind her firmly.

"Help me, Daddy," Yeo-deol breathed urgently, the yellow button-up shirt hanging off her shoulder.

"Couldn't this have waited, sweetie? It's very late, and you should know better than to be beating down the doors like that," Daddy said, taking off his glasses with a frown. He looked so much paler than she remembered him, like he had caught the maids' sickness.

Yeo-deol walked to his desk, waiting for him to notice. For him to notice her face slick in sweat, her hands bloodied in splinters, the bruises darkening along her arms and legs. She waited for Daddy to leap into a fury and ask what was wrong, who did this, that he would kill Auntie and revive her sisters heroically.

But her real Daddy remained seated, his tilted head barely indulging her distress and pale eyes reflecting the dust-choked room. The aching empathy of his tears, the willingness to draw her pink elephants, the simple acts of spending time with her, it had all dried up now that Yeo-deol was no longer on the brink of death.

Each and every one of you is Mama to me.

Something dried up in Yeo-deol too.

No. Daddy, I'm Yeo-deol.

Yeo-deol had to take a step back as the study seemed to shrink around Daddy's smothering gray eyes. In this act of distancing, she blinked and saw that his paleness was actually a thick covering of dust accumulating over him in floating particles. Raising out her own arms, she saw there was a lighter covering over her own skin.

How long had the dust been gradually burying their house?

Perhaps since her first inhale of dusty air the night Auntie appeared and almost took away her breath. Yeo-deol remembered the naked Mama's deadened eyes, though, and she couldn't blame everything on Auntie. Perhaps the dust had begun to fall from further back, before Mama had disappeared and they had seemed to live happy lives. Outside this room, the house was crumbling apart and becoming undone.

Yeo-deol thought about the empty chair at the dining table.

"Yeo-deol?" Daddy asked, still waiting, but his blinks were growing languid.

A peace enveloped Yeo-deol's heart. After this, she would join her sisters and bow her head with them. But first, she wanted to tell Daddy everything she had seen and learned about Mama. This would be her last gift to him.

"I've had dreams that kept going and going," Yeo-deol began. *They're disintegrating now.*

"I see Mama in them. She's the happiest I've seen her." *… apart from you, Daddy.*

"Mama's connected to a man named Dong-ju. If you split them apart, they'll become cracked apart." *Not like how you found a substitute for Mama in Auntie.*

"I had a ninth sister before Ahop named Gippeum, meaning happiness."

Mama said no more, but she ended up having two more.

"I think Mama was really tired, Daddy."

She wasn't inside her body anymore.

"The dream led me here to you, one last time. It's just you and me left in this house. Everyone else is gone now, and I didn't want you to wait here forever." … *choking in this dust.*

"Let's go together, Daddy," Yeo-deol said, extending her hand. They could go to the dining room together and join her sisters and Mama.

Daddy's eyes had grown wide as Yeo-deol talked. The frozen look was too wide, too hardened to be from the apprehension or amazement for which she had hoped. His mouth was stuffed with something hard again, but this time, he had the force to spit out what was bared between his teeth: "That whore. Whore, whore, whore."

He had latched onto the wrong part of Yeo-deol's dream.

"Who will love me? Who will redeem me?" Daddy slumped into his chair.

"I can love you, Daddy," Yeo-deol said, not quite understanding what he was talking about. She tugged at his shoulders, her eyes fixed to the cracks that were running across the ceiling. But Daddy couldn't seem to see that she was right in front of him.

The torrent of dust broke through the ceiling in a column that swallowed up Daddy. No matter how much Yeo-deol sifted her hands through the cascade of dust, she couldn't find him anymore, as if he had disintegrated into dust.

CHAPTER 14

——

Yeo-deol covered her eyes with the flat of her hands.

I will not cry.

I will not cry.

I will not cry.

Mama and her sisters had disappeared like tricks of the air, here one moment and gone the next. Daddy had died in front of her, his agape mouth and widening eyes taking in the torrent of dust with a final look of horror. He had asked who would love him, not remembering his ten daughters who had been created to love him, not hearing the one who had answered him.

Before she let herself cry, she would find Auntie.

When Yeo-deol opened the door, the mass of her sisters' dark hair launched into the room and engulfed Daddy's study. She relaxed into the slithering of the hair that smelled like her sisters, not knowing why she had tried to escape it in the first place. The hair was an extension of her sisters, and they all, in turn, were embedded into this house.

Cocooned inside the mass of hair, Yeo-deol focused on drawing out the kitchen in her mind: the ceiling-to-floor curtain of spices, the lock in the wall behind it, and the opening door. The mass of her sisters' hair rolled away and gently set Yeo-deol onto the dusty floor of the kitchen facing the curtain of spices. Her pillowcase was by her leg. To the side, a maid was folded over on a stainless steel table, breaking down into dust particles that wafted into the heavy air.

Yeo-deol parted the curtains and opened the door.

Auntie sat in the dark with her head lowered over her knees. She didn't move as Yeo-deol tucked back the long black hair touching the floor and pushed the tip of the fountain pen into the base of her neck. The skin discolored in a blotch of purple as the poisonous ink traveled through her bloodstream. Auntie's head bobbed down a little, and her arms fell away limply.

Yeo-deol sat down next to Auntie and set the uncapped pen between the two of them.

"I'm sorry," Auntie said, twisting her head to Yeo-deol.

The huge tears slicking down from her hazel eyes were reminiscent of honey. Yeo-deol stared at this woman, who looked nothing like the gnarled, twisted witches of fairy tales.

"Did it hurt for my sisters?" Yeo-deol asked.

Auntie feebly swayed her head in a "no" over her chills.

"I gave them their heart's desires, and they were content," she said.

"That was it? My sisters died because they were *satisfied*?"

"You have to be alive in order to die," Auntie said, "You girls were created by your mother's will, and separated from your mother, I made your sisters happy enough to rest."

It didn't particularly surprise Yeo-deol to hear that she and her sisters weren't entirely real. *Like can see like.* They had always loved being Mama's shadows. She had seen into the pink room, where Gippeum had been the baby Mama had failed to create out of her happiness.

"You're not alive either," Yeo-deol said, "not if you were born in the snow as an adult."

"I was created to be your new Mama by your Mama," Auntie said through her blue lips.

"Were we that bad that you had to put us to rest?" Yeo-deol asked quietly.

"Of course not. I adored my girls from the beginning. But your Daddy, he suffocated me. He degraded me as a mere copy of your Mama. He punished me for your Mama's disappearance." Auntie was struggling to talk.

Yeo-deol helped ease Auntie onto the ground as the body convulsions began.

"I kept on wondering for how much longer must I suffer like this?" Auntie said finally.

She didn't suffer for long on the ground, at least.

"You can go back to the snow now," Yeo-deol said, clos-ing Auntie's eyes, which had leached to a glassy white. She pressed a kiss on each eyelid, wishing her a safe journey back.

Dragging the pillowcase behind her, Yeo-deol had no desti-nation in mind as she walked out into the snow. There was no rush to return since everyone else was gone now. She would join her sisters after taking one more walk.

As the snow deepened to her waist, Yeo-deol lifted the pillowcase above her head and continued wading into the dark-ened forest from where Auntie had emerged to enter their house. Now she was emerging from her house to enter Auntie's forest.

The thick canopy of trees cast a pitch-black darkness around Yeo-deol that was relieved only by the illumination from the ground of snow she walked on. Yeo-deol followed a distinctive streak that ran through the snow. She walked for a while, humming a distant Korean lullaby about a baby that had been left to be lulled by the ocean. The streak ended at black brass gates marked by a wooden sign with red squiggles.

It was a house, in the middle of the woods.

Yeo-deol pushed the gate open and entered. Above her, the trees had given away to a clear square of sky punctuated by a full moon. The naked Mama from the last supper sat on mossy cement steps leading up to the front door of the house. Her figure was softened by the moonlight that dipped onto her bare shoulders. She balanced a pink frosted cake in her lap with holes where the candles had been.

"Hi, Mama," Yeo-deol said, dropping her pillowcase to the ground.

She burst into the tears she had been holding back.

The naked Mama pulled Yeo-deol onto her lap, closing her in securely with her arms as her Mama had done countless times.

"Don't cry, you did so well," Mama said.

Yeo-deol shook her head because she hadn't done well in anything.

"Everyone is gone now, Mama, this is the end," Yeo-deol said, feeling her eyes grow heavier. Maybe this was her contentment. She was slipping back into the shadows, back into the part of Mama she had been created from. But Mama jostled her awake.

"No, you and your sisters are strong. All dreams come to an end eventually, but you and your sisters are going to leave the house."

Leave the house? Yeo-deol couldn't fathom the possibility.

"Will you leave the house with us?" Yeo-deol asked softly, though she already knew the answer in Mama's arms wrapping around her tightly.

"Yeo-deol, both life and dreams eat away at you until you've scattered pieces of yourself everywhere. You get to choose a core, essential part of yourself to hold onto, though. Mine became regret."

Mama turned to the darkened house behind them. The peeling paint of the front door, the sun-bleached brick, the outcropping of weeds indicated that several decades had passed since the house had been lived in.

"My regret is here, in dreams, in all the layers I've been creating. Now I need to lay with them. But oh, my beautiful girls, the house I created is too small for you. I'll make sure you girls can leave the house, but you need to choose good, worthwhile things to hold onto."

Mama looked so sad, shivering in the chill of the night. Disentangling herself from Mama's lap, Yeo-deol unbuttoned her yellow shirt and draped it over Mama, who seemed to recognize it as she touched the fabric almost tenderly. After transferring the white sneakers to Mama's feet, Yeo-deol handed over the pillowcase containing the underwear, still sun-warm to the touch, as well as the baby blanket.

"Why are you giving me these things?"

"These are for you, from all the other dream Mamas. They aren't all as sad as you believe. We'll be strong, Mama, since you're our core. You did well as our Mama too."

Mama brought up her hands over her eyes. She was covering her tears, Yeo-deol realized.

"You just have to walk through two more doorways, and then you'll wake up," Mama said.

Pressing a kiss to Mama's wet cheek, Yeo-deol went up the stairs and opened the door to the house. As she stepped through the doorway, she allowed herself to look back one last time. Mama's face was crumpled in unabashed crying as the sky lightened into dawn. In the distance, she could hear the engine of an approaching car. But Mama smiled as she cupped her hands around her mouth and yelled into the morning, "Thank you for being my daughter."

Inside the house, the orange tree was rooted before Yeo-deol with its burgundy trunk and split middle resembling splayed legs. There were ten oranges in the tree again, although she had picked off ten the first time. The first ten oranges had weighed down the branches with their weight, but this time, there was only one orange that loomed in size over the other oranges, as big as a grapefruit or a baby's head. Yeo-deol's orange. It was ready for her.

The tree's trunk was slumped in a slight bend that suggested it was losing strength, which could be seen in the acrid yellow of the branch tips. The tree wasn't dead yet but would take years to waste away, waiting for the nine other oranges to ripen. Perhaps Yeo-deol would have to wait awhile for her other sisters to wake up.

Yeo-deol stretched out both her hands under the swollen orange. She had no heart to climb the sick tree. The tree groaned, quaking the ground below Yeo-deol. *Pop.* The orange plopped into Yeo-deol's hands. Blood dripped from the stem it fell from. *Dugun... Dugun...Dugun...*

"Thank you, Mama." Yeo-deol bit into the orange.

When she opened her eyes, she was in the turret, where her sisters were laid out in their sleeping spots, their skin and hair turned back to normal. In Yeo-deol's arms was the pillowcase stuffed full of nine ripened oranges, Mama's last gift for the girls.

ACKNOWLEDGEMENTS

Even having reached this point, I can't quite seem to grasp that I am publishing a book. I still don't feel that I deserve it. Quite often, it devolved into sitting on the floor and saying, "I can't do this." But I could do it, only because of the family, friends, teachers, and acquaintances who supported me through writing and then publishing *Yellow Boxes*. Thank you, to each and every one of you, for allowing me to be able to do this once.

Thank you first and foremost to my family: my mother, who always reminds me I am more than my accomplishments and failures; my father, who teaches me to be gentle; my sister, who believes in me ferociously, hand-in-hand with her husband and my brother-in-law; my brother, who made it rain candy when I wanted to cry the most.

Thank you to all my friends, who warmed my heart with their excitement for my book, bigger than I imagined.

I sent way too many Snapchats of my process, forgive me — especially to Karen and Amy, who often fielded by 2 a.m. meltdowns via text.

Thank you to Karen again, and Mr. Terich, my high school English teacher, who took their time to give me feedback on partial Advanced Reader Copies of *Yellow Boxes*. I know I wasn't able to address everything that was brought up, but I am grateful for the depth of thought and effort you put into the feedback I received.

Thank you to Mairead Case, author of *See You in the Morning*, with whom I had the privilege to correspond before setting out to write this story and after, in my pre-ordering campaign. Your words of affirmation and willingness to talk gave me courage, knowing someone out there believed in me as a writer.

Thank you to New Degree Press, especially Eric Koester, Brian Bies, Shelby Hogan, Elina Oliferovskiy, Amanda Brown, and Agata Wawryniuk. You were my village, even if I was mostly a lost child frolicking with the sheep — thank you for your patience with me, and allowing me to keep a sheep or two of my own.

And finally, thank you to everyone who took part in my pre-ordering campaign for *Yellow Boxes*, whether it was by contributions or helping spread the word. You made publishing this book in the first place possible. Thank you, from the bottom of my heart, for helping me accomplish one of my greatest dreams.

Eric Koester

Amy Gulley*

Bobae Cho

Jessica Li

Shahbaz Ahmed Khan

Zaki Mahmoud

Justin Park

Lily Do

Leslie Fisher

Jeremiah Kim

Andrew Daniel Baker

Robert E. Abrams

Kitty Li

Katie Brandao*

Celia Manne*

Terrance Terich

Brian Dang

Angelica Runstadler

Yoojoo Lim

Sita Manne

Jill Chang

Liz Han

Laura Martin

Ana Rodriguez-Knutsen

Sarah Park*

Regan Colburn

Jason Lee

Shawn Lee Chang

Rosemary Jones

Diane L. Dorsey

Karen Lee

Jeffrey Frace

Suzanne Houghton

Yris Eang

Elisa Truong

Rebecca Talbot-Bluechel

Lu-Fang Hung

Tawan Maneenil

Julie Hwang

Rebecca Ta

Christine Wysong*

Hanna Kim You*

Mikaela Schilling

Sabrina Lu

Yunghoon Yeo

Aubrey Unemori

Diana Davidson

Lauren Ho

Allison Brown

Josh Junsuk Ko

Seungheon Lee

John Cho

Seolryu Hwang

Suzzy Ahn

Eun Joo Lee

Sara Bahten

Yung Suk Han*

Kristine Ly

Key: *multiple copies

www.ingramcontent.com/pod-product-compliance
Lightning Source LLC
Chambersburg PA
CBHW071521180526
45171CB00002B/338